WHY
ERA
FAILED

EVERYWOMAN: Studies in History,
Literature, and Culture

Susan Gubar and Joan Hoff-Wilson
General Editors

Mary Frances Berry

WHY
ERA
FAILED

POLITICS, WOMEN'S RIGHTS, AND THE AMENDING PROCESS OF THE CONSTITUTION

INDIANA UNIVERSITY PRESS
BLOOMINGTON • INDIANAPOLIS

First Midland Book Edition 1988

© 1986 by Mary Frances Berry

All rights reserved

Manufactured in the United States of America

Library of Congress Cataloging-in-Publication Data

Berry, Mary Frances.
Why ERA failed.

(Everywoman : studies in history, literature, and culture)
Bibliography: p.
Includes index.
1. Equal rights amendments—United States.   2. Women—
Legal status, laws, etc.—United States.   3. Women's
rights—United States. I. Title. II. Series:
Everywoman.
KF4758.B45   1986   342.73′0878′02632   85-45985

cl.ISBN   0-253-36537-6
pa.ISBN   0-253-20459-3

2 3 4 5 6   92 91 90 89 88 87

CONTENTS

Preface

The purpose of this book is to analyze why ERA failed in the context of the history of the amending process of the Constitution. The genesis of the book lies in my dismay as I testified before the House Judiciary Committee concerning ERA. I noticed that there was so little discussion on the traditional principle of the equality of rights and so much on whether ERA would violate traditional family values. Creating an appearance that some essential values would be compromised by adding an amendment is a powerful weapon that cannot easily be defused. This strategy had been used before by those opposed to a proposed amendment. Because the Constitution is by design more difficult to amend than not, I believe it would be useful to present an explanation of the inherent difficulties of the amending process in order to understand the outcome of the ERA controversy.

Acknowledgments

So many people helped me as I researched and wrote this book that it would be impossible to list them all. The students in my Constitutional History and History of American Law classes at Howard University asked penetrating questions and shared startling insights. My graduate assistant Joseph Windham helped with the research, and my colleague Eileen Boris read some of the material and helped immeasurably. Francis C. Haber of the University of Maryland, College Park, read the manuscript and was my best critic.

The scholars and students gathered at the Sixth Berkshire Conference on Women's History listened to and criticized a paper I gave on this subject as a keynote address before I had written the book. Jane DeHart Mathews and Donald Mathews let me read some of their unpublished material, and Blanche Wiesen Cook talked to me about many issues, including Eleanor Roosevelt's views on ERA.

Joan Hoff-Wilson was the very best of editors, and the people at Indiana University Press were superb in producing this work in record time.

Talking and listening to Phyllis Schlafly, Eleanor Smeal, Judy Goldsmith, Kathy Wilson, Judy Lichtman, Shirley Chisholm, the late Pauli Murray, Addie Wyatt, C. Delores Tucker, Blandina Cardenas Ramirez, Donna Brazile, Gloria Toote, Antoinette Ford, and a number of other remarkable women helped enormously.

Elizabeth Abramowitz, T. J. Davis, and, as always, Minerva Hawkins and my mother, Frances Berry Wiggins, gave me warm and persistent encouragement.

Without Linda Edwards I would not have been able to finish this book or anything else I have written.

MFB

WHY
ERA
FAILED

Introduction

Increasingly the prospects for the addition of an Equal Rights Amendment to the Constitution seem dismal. Proponents seem to be losing instead of gaining ground in the Congress and in a sufficient number of states. In a *New York Times* poll announced on November 27, 1983, when reminded that ERA had failed of ratification, 54 percent of the men but only 48 percent of the women believed it was "important that another effort be made to ratify" it.[1] A poll published in *Parade* magazine on March 4, 1984, after ERA had been voted down in the House of Representatives, reported that women's first three concerns were (1) equal pay for equal work, (2) equal rights in general, (3) job discrimination. The Equal Rights Amendment was only in sixth place on their list. Abortion was higher, in fourth place.[2] The results of these polls, if they have any validity, combined with the failure to achieve enough ratification states in 1982 and the rejection of ERA by the House of Representatives in 1983, indicate that ERA proponents have failed to convince a majority of women in enough states that ERA is essential to the implementation of their concerns about equal rights and to dispel their fears that ERA would make other changes in their lives that they did not desire.

The failure of the Equal Rights Amendment ratification effort had many causes. This study considers only the behavior of the ERA proponents and opponents compared with that of participants in earlier ratification campaigns for controversial proposed amendments to the federal Constitution. It describes the history of the amending process from the Constitutional Convention to the present day and its application to struggles over amendments concerned with the status of blacks after the Civil War, the income tax, Prohibition, child labor, and woman suffrage. Other than the Civil War amendments, these were initiated during a period of populist and progressive reform dating from about 1890 to the entry of the United States into World War I. The Populists, primarily discontented Western and Southern agrarians, wanted political participation by women, monetary reform, and governmental regulation of monopolies and an income tax instead of high tariffs. Drawing upon the populist legacy, progressivism, a mostly urban, middle-class response to the evils of rapid industrialization, supported Prohibition, women's rights, the abolition of child labor, and income tax.

The amendments selected were chosen because they best demonstrate the problems inherent in trying to achieve ratification for proposals that are designed to make major substantive change in aspects of American life, such as that attempted by ERA supporters. Six other amendments that were adopted were not included in this study be-

1

cause at the time they were proposed they were regarded as primarily making technical or procedural changes in the functioning of government. These six amendments provided for direct election of senators instead of by state legislatures, limited the president to two terms, allowed District of Columbia residents to vote in presidential elections, prohibited poll taxes in federal elections, regulated presidential succession, and gave eighteen-year-olds the right to vote.

The careful building of a structure to provide for change but to protect the integrity of the Constitution from inappropriate proposals can be seen in the debates at the Constitutional Convention over the amending power. As a result, amendments could be proposed by the states or the Congress, but to gain approval and ratification they needed definitive majority support at each stage of the process. The framers established as the essential requirement for success a general sentiment and belief that constitutional change was necessary, characterized in this study as consensus. However, the consensus had to be achieved both nationally and separately in the states to gain ratification.

From the earliest amendments before the Civil War and Reconstruction, only a little wisdom can be garnered concerning what will happen when a controversial change is proposed. Therefore, a consideration of the first twelve amendments is included only to elaborate the successful working of the process as public confidence in its efficacy was reinforced. The Bill of Rights, the first ten amendments, achieved easy ratification, as did the eleventh and twelfth, which dealt with relatively uncontroversial matters.

The history of the thirteenth, fourteenth, and fifteenth amendments, by contrast, illustrates a pattern for the passage of amendments that affirmed major changes in the society. Change occurred, as the framers intended, but it took time and overwhelming evidence that resolution could not come within the perimeters of the existing Constitution. The income tax amendment and the woman suffrage amendment followed a similar pattern but also demonstrated the importance of developing state-by-state support first as an impulse to change. The Prohibition amendment reinforced the earlier experience regarding what was required for success. In addition, however, the history of Prohibition demonstrated the consequences of having only artificial support for a symbolic amendment instead of real support for a change in law and policy. Repeal came more swiftly than enactment.

The child labor amendment was a special case. It would have made a major change in American life, but it was not ratified. Its failure demonstrated most clearly the result when neither an artificial nor a real majority sentiment can be demonstrated in the states at the right

time. It also showed how important it was for amendment supporters
to decide whether what they wanted to accomplish could be done
without an amendment. Ultimately the regulation they wanted was
achieved without amending the Constitution.

From the history of earlier controversial amendments before ERA,
a pattern became clear. In order to achieve ratification, there had to
be a perception among a majority of voters in most congressional
districts and states that a societal problem existed that had not been
remedied by the courts, legislatures, or the Congress, and which could
be solved only if the Constitution were changed. A perception about
the urgency of the problem had to be conveyed to legislators and the
Congress with such force that they feared a negative reaction at the
polls from a majority of voters if they did not act. The case for the
amendment had to be made in such defensible terms that legislators
felt safe in defending themselves against opponents. Most importantly, tactics and strategy to meet these objectives could not be *just*
national. They had to address regional variations and geographic differences within a state. In addition, the more substantive the change
encompassed in an amendment, the more likely that passage would
require considerable time—decades rather than years.

If the analysis in this study is correct, ERA approval was problematic
at best and defeat predictable. Supporters did too little, too late of
what is required for ratification of a substantive proposal. Furthermore, the number of state ratifications was deceptive. Support was
eroding instead of increasing in the final stages of the campaign.

The Early History of the Constitutional Amendment Process

1

In the period of American history before the end of Reconstruction, various political issues stimulated proposed amendments to the Constitution, but only fifteen were adopted. These successfully negotiated a process that was deliberately made difficult. The framers made amending the federal Constitution possible because they did not want to leave revolution as the only route for constitutional change in the new nation. Experience with trying to gain unanimity to amend the Articles of Confederation led them to provide a process of amendment that did not require the votes of all the states, as required under the Articles. However, they balanced the need for amendment with the necessity for maintaining stability in the new federal system under the Constitution. Therefore, they required both substantial national agreement as well as agreement among most of the states. They mandated consensus, based on necessity, which was understood as a perception at the time an amendment is proposed that nothing but constitutional change can solve an outstanding problem that must be remedied in the national interest. To implement the process, a public, lawful expression of consensus for change had to be demonstrated through a super-majority vote, consisting of a two-thirds majority in each house of the Congress, and separate majority support of more than 50 percent in the legislatures or conventions of three-fourths of the states. They also permitted proposals for amendments to be initiated by two-thirds of the states calling for a convention for the purpose.[1]

The Constitutional Convention spent a great deal of time on the various features of the new Constitution, but in light of their experiences and hopes, it is clear that the process of constitutional amendment was a major issue for the delegates. On May 29, 1787, Edmund Randolph of Virginia proposed that provision be made to amend the Constitution whenever necessary without national legislative approval.

In addition, Charles Pinckney of South Carolina proposed a draft constitution, including an amendment process. He suggested that when two-thirds of the legislatures asked the national legislature to call a convention for amendments, it should do so, or in the alternative, the Congress by a two-thirds vote of both houses might propose and two-thirds of the legislatures might adopt amendments.[2]

But, curiously, when Randolph's draft was discussed on June 5, 1787, Pinckney asserted that "provision for amending the Constitution should not be made. The propriety and necessity of it are doubtful." Others did not agree with him. Elbridge Gerry of Massachusetts, for example, pointed out that in the eight states that had amending clauses in their constitutions, "nothing had yet happened . . . to prove its impropriety."[3]

The Convention, wanting to provide a mode of amendment, agonized over what respective roles the states and Congress should play. Gerry of Massachusetts feared that if two-thirds of the states could insure a convention, they might "subvert the State constitutions altogether." He did not want any number of states to be able to do anything that might require changes in the constitution of a particular state without its consent. Hamilton did not agree with Gerry, but he feared that if the only amendment procedure was to have the states propose a convention, "The State legislatures will not apply for alterations but with a view to increase their own powers." He wanted the Congress, also, to be empowered to call a convention. Madison thought having a convention without saying whether it would propose amendments or adopt them was too vague. Roger Sherman wanted Congress to be able to propose amendments but wanted the consent of all states required for adoption. As the discussion continued, Madison proposed the basic method of amendment, dividing responsibility between the states and the Congress, which is now in the Constitution as adopted.[4]

Madison explained the reasons why the Convention had included a provision for amendments as follows:

> That useful alterations will be suggested by experience could not but be foreseen. It was requisite therefore that a mode for introducing them should be provided. The mode preferred by the Convention seems to be stamped with every mark of propriety. It guards equally against that extreme facility which would render the Constitution too mutable; and that extreme difficulty which might perpetuate its discovered faults.[5]

Although the provision for states to require the calling of a national constitutional convention has not been used, the framers exercised great foresight in adopting an amendment process. Numerous changes have been proposed but few have been adopted, and the basic structure of republican government under the Constitution has withstood the test of time. From the adoption of Article V to the present, about 5,000 amendments to the Constitution have been proposed, but only twenty-six have been added, and only six others have been adopted by Congress but failed of ratification. One of these, which would give voting representation to the District of Columbia in Congress, is currently before the states; and the ERA, having failed of ratification, is again before the Congress.[6]

The ten earliest amendments, which make up the Bill of Rights, arose directly from public rejection of the convention delegates' decision to exclude protection for certain fundamental freedoms in the new Constitution. Many people were not convinced that such matters as freedom of expression and protection from a lack of due process in criminal cases did not need to be insulated from attack by the new government. The Convention had rejected after brief consideration a proposal by Elbridge Gerry and George Mason for a Bill of Rights. Alexander Hamilton explained later that bills of rights were needed when subjects wrested privileges from kings, but the Constitution flowed from the power of the people and "as they retain everything, they have no need of particular reservations."[7]

Despite the continuing arguments of Hamilton and the Convention against a Bill of Rights, in the state ratifying conventions more than 200 amendments were proposed to remedy perceived defects in the document. Of these, 124 were proposed by seven of the states as absolutely necessary to protect civil liberties under the new Constitution. Proponents of the Constitution were forced to promise their enactment to defuse opposition and to assure the votes for successful ratification. To keep these promises, James Madison, early in the first Congress, introduced a series of provisions embodying the proposed amendments.[8]

After a long debate, seventeen amendments passed the House by the necessary two-thirds majority, but two of these were rejected by the Senate. One would have protected citizens from state infringement of the rights of trial by jury, conscience, freedom of speech, and freedom of the press. It was rejected, based on the rationale that the purpose of a Bill of Rights was to protect citizens only against encroachments by the national government. They could, through state governmental processes, decide what protections they needed against their own state governments. The other rejected amendment would have insured that neither branch of government would violate separation of powers by trying to exercise the functions of another branch. The Senate believed sufficient insurance against that problem was assured by the clear distinctions among the Judiciary, Congress, and the Executive in the Constitution itself. After the remaining amendments were consolidated into twelve, they were voted out to the states by the requisite two-thirds majorities. Excluding two amendments limiting the number of representatives and fixing the compensation of members of Congress, they were ratified by each of the states, except Georgia, Connecticut, and Massachusetts, and became the first additions to the new Constitution.[9]

Two other amendments were added to the Constitution in this early period of our national life. The eleventh, occasioned by a suit against Georgia by a citizen of another state, prevented the Judiciary from hearing such suits against a state; and the twelfth provided for Senate elections for President and Vice-President, after the tied vote in the election of 1800. The eleventh gained easy approval because the assumption of jurisdiction by the federal courts in such a case was regarded as a violation of the inherent constitutional principle of divided sovereignty between the states and the federal government. An undoubted consensus existed for its passage. The vote in the Senate was 23–2 and in the House 81–9. All the states, except Pennsylvania and New York, quickly ratified.[10]

The Twelfth Amendment arose because the hastily drawn electoral college provision, which was tossed in as an afterthought at the Constitutional Convention, created the procedural difficulty of having a President and Vice-President of the same party receive an equal number of votes. The House had to choose between Aaron Burr and Thomas Jefferson in 1801, when Burr refused to defer, although knowing he had been nominated for Vice-President. The amendment, by requiring separate slates and votes for each office in the electoral college, solved the problem. The Twelfth Amendment received less support than the Eleventh primarily because the Federalists preferred to preserve any opportunity for creating political mischief for the Republicans during their ascendency after Jefferson's election. In the House, the amendment passed twice, the second time by a vote of 84–42. After failing by one vote on the first attempt in the Senate, it passed, but only by 22–10. Only Massachusetts, Delaware, and Connecticut voted not to ratify. They thought it would encourage the development of political parties, which they regarded as "unwise, impolitic, and unconstitutional."[11]

Between 1804 and 1860, some 400 constitutional amendments were introduced in the Congress, usually on whatever was the hot political topic of the day. Such issues as internal improvements at national expense, the national bank question, Federalist opposition to the War of 1812, the slavery question, and nullification crisis, all resulted in the introduction of amendments in one house of Congress. Only one amendment gained a national consensus: a provision that anyone who accepted a title of nobility without the consent of Congress, or a present, office, or emolument from a foreign sovereign or state would lose his citizenship and be incapable of holding office in the United States. It passed the House by a vote of 87–3 and the Senate by 16–5. It failed of ratification by only one vote. New York, Connecticut, South Carolina, and Rhode Island voted against it. Virginia's action was not reported. Of three amendments concerned with election of electors by districts, choice of representatives, and no third presidential term, two passed the Senate but not the House. All of these arose because of continued dissatisfaction and disputes over presidential elections. In this early period, congressmen showed a great penchant for introducing amendments, but consistent with the framers' intentions, change in the fundamental structure of government was not easily achieved.[12]

The slavery issue and the Civil War brought the next set of successful amendments to the Constitution. Amendments had been introduced repeatedly to end slavery or protect it in the period before the Civil War, but only after more than fifty years of discussion did secession and the war create a sufficient perception of necessity and the achievement of consensus in the North on the issue.

In the *Dred Scott* decision of 1857, the Supreme Court had foreclosed the possibility of congressional action to limit the expansion of slavery in the territories. When the election of the new Republican party's candidate, Abraham Lincoln, led to Southern secession out of fear that slavery would be undermined in the South, the resulting war to save the Union led to constitutional change. On June 19, 1862, President Lincoln signed a bill abolishing slavery in the territories despite the *Dred Scott* decision. Also, Lincoln's Emancipation Proclamation of 1863 had provided freedom for the war's duration to some slaves, but the Proclamation was based legally on the Civil War powers, which were in doubt once hostilities ended. Furthermore, many slaves were still being held legally in the border slave states. With military victory increasingly in sight, it was clear that some new determination of the legal status of millions of blacks, thousands of whom were serving in the Union Army, had to be made. The practical difficulty of re-enslaving blacks, many of whom were armed, and the moral and political unacceptability of re-establishing a system of servitude or of conceding that the new law prohibiting slavery in territories was null because of the *Dred Scott* case, created a perception that it was necessary to make a new arrangement. The only way the *Dred Scott* decision could really be overturned without legal conflict, in the absence of a reversal by the Supreme Court, was by constitutional amendment.[13]

In April 1864, with the Southern states not in the Union and therefore no barrier to action, the perception of necessity led the Senate to vote 38–6 to approve the Thirteenth Amendment abolishing slavery. In January 1865, the House followed suit, voting 119–56 to approve the amendment. By December 1865, enough consensus existed in three-fourths of the states in the Union (including eight formerly in the Confederacy that were not recognized for other purposes) to gain ratification and the amendment was declared approved. By its terms neither slavery nor involuntary servitude could ever exist in the states or in the territories or places subject to United States jurisdiction.[14]

But the end of slavery and its permanent exclusion from the territories left untouched that part of the *Dred Scott* decision which seemed to bar United States citizenship for blacks. Congress, in determining what status the newly freed blacks should have, enacted the Civil Rights Act of 1866 to provide citizenship and the right to hold property, to sue and be sued, and other rights that had been denied to slaves. But the Congress recognized that a statute does not repeal a Supreme Court decision based on constitutional grounds, just as a statute can be overturned by a later decision that it is unconstitutional. In addition, although the hostilities had officially ended, thousands of blacks were still in the Union Army, whites were demanding to go home and were being mustered out rapidly, and now white Southerners seemed unwilling to accord blacks citizenship rights. These conditions created a perception that another constitutional amendment was necessary to overturn *Dred Scott*'s denial of citizenship to blacks. For this purpose, Congress, in June 1866, passed the Fourteenth Amendment by a vote of 33–11 in the Senate and 120–32 in the House. Enough consensus was gained for ratification, in part by requiring Southern states to ratify the amendment as a condition for readmission to the Union. Because of concern that the Fourteenth Amendment did not clearly protect the right of blacks to vote, and because their vote was needed if the Republican party was to have an opportunity to compete in the South, and also to protect black voting in the North from legislative denial, dominant Republicans perceived the necessity for another constitutional amendment. In the 1868 election, newly enfranchised freedmen in the seven already reconstructed Southern states helped to elect President Grant by a narrow margin, but many blacks in Louisiana and Georgia had been prevented from voting. The Fifteenth Amendment prohibiting the denial of the right to vote on the grounds of race, which passed the Senate 39–13 and the House 145–49 when Congress reconvened in 1864, was ratified by three-fourths of the states in 1870. This was the last constitutional amendment adopted in the nineteenth century.[15]

Ultimately, undoing the right of slave owners to possess slave property perpetually, which was one of the essential compromises of the original Constitution, came only with force of arms. In the events leading to the war, there were sufficient reasons for Northerners to be willing to abolish slavery. The institution existed principally in the South, although Northern manufacturers derived indirect benefits from trade and the utilization of Southern agricultural products. In addition, there were strong economic incentives for Northerners, who did not like competing with unfree labor, to oppose the slave power even if they were not in principle opposed to slavery. But in the absence of the war in the North, there was not a sufficient perception of necessity or of a possibility for the kind of consensus that is the essential substance from which constitutional change emerges. In the South, faced with the option of perpetuating the political crisis created by the Union victory, politicians perceived an urgent necessity for readmission and the possibility of readjustment. This perception created enough consensus among those who had the power to act to ratify the Civil War amendments.

From the nineteenth-century excursion into amendment-making, some clear patterns developed. The provision for amendments initiated by an application of two-thirds of the states lay dormant, but congressmen found amendment proposing to be a helpful political tool. Amendments could be easily proposed, but the stringent requirements of a two-thirds majority in the Congress and three-fourths of the states prevented precipitous action.

Procedural problems in the very structure of the Constitution, such as the sloppily drafted electoral college system or the assumption of jurisdiction by federal courts in ways unintended, could be remedied without too much difficulty. But deeply felt substantive matters such as the slavery issue lingered and festered long before an overpowering sense of necessity achieved consensus. Some compelling impetus had to stimulate the approval of such far-reaching changes in governmental policy. The experience also demonstrated that quick discouragement by proponents is ahistorical when an amendment is substantive. The enormous constitutional change of ending slavery took fifty-seven years from its first introduction in the House before the Thirteenth Amendment ending slavery was ratified.

Adopting an Income Tax: The Sixteenth Amendment 2

More than fifty years passed between the Civil War amendments and the next major substantive change in the Constitution—the income tax amendment. The struggle over the amendment's approval exhibited the essential characteristics of the process as outlined by the Constitution's framers. Overwhelming majority opinion in favor of passage was a long time in coming. The proposed path was so difficult because it projected a major substantive change in the mode of financing expenditures of the national government, but its adoption made further expansion of federal responsibilities possible. Time for extended debate and the negative effects of a Supreme Court decision, as in the case of the Civil War amendments, led to a developing consensus in the states which created the climate of opinion necessary for passage. The history of its inception and final approval provides additional information about the process for adopting a highly controversial proposal.

The ratification of the Sixteenth Amendment on February 25, 1913, giving Congress the power "to lay and collect taxes on income, from whatever source derived, without apportionment among the several States, and without regard to any census or enumeration," followed a difficult path to success. The American people had a history of unpleasant experiences with taxes dating from the colonial period. The British government provided for colonial defense but exacted revenue from the settlers through a series of tariffs and excises. The colonists had modest internal expenditures. Little was spent on public works or social welfare, and only a few colonies supported the church by taxation. When revenue was needed, the poll tax, the faculty tax, or the property tax came into use along with excises and duties on commerce between and among the colonies. While the poll tax was exacted from each individual and the excise was a sales tax on certain goods, the faculty tax on assumed earnings and profits was a forerunner of the income tax. First used in the colony of New Plymouth in 1643, it taxed the colonists "according to their estates or faculties." The faculty tax idea spread not only throughout New England but to several of the southern colonies. In South Carolina and Massachusetts such a tax existed up to the Civil War.[1]

The Revolutionary War placed increased pressure on the colonial system of taxation. Colonists had great difficulty in translating the rhetoric of gaining independence into the reality of paying for the war. Paper money, requisitions, foreign subsidies, and domestic and foreign loans provided an unreliable source of funds. The government under the Articles of Confederation could not levy a national tariff without the unanimous consent of the states. In addition to borrowing, the government could requisition states in proportion to the value of their land and improvements. But without a loan from France, the war might have been lost for a lack of funds. The army suffered horribly from time to time as the army commanders made requisitions to the states but little was forthcoming.[2]

These experiences with revenue problems led the Constitutional Convention to give Congress the power to lay and collect taxes, duties, imports, and excises, to pay the debts and provide for the common defense and general welfare of the United States. Seven state ratifying conventions proposed amendments to prohibit the federal government from levying a direct or capitation tax unless in proportion to the census. Concerned about the federal government acting independently, they wanted Congress to be forced, when income was insufficient to cover expenses, to make requisitions upon the states before laying direct taxes. The Constitution required that direct taxes must be apportioned among the several states according to their populations. Direct taxes were not explicitly defined in the early years under the Constitution although the Supreme Court decided that at least a tax on carriages was not a direct tax. Congress imposed a direct tax five times to raise revenue reapportioned according to the census in 1798, 1813, 1815, 1816, and 1861.[3]

The issue of federal power to tax became an urgent matter again in the nineteenth century. Before the Civil War, tariffs on imports and revenues from land sales provided the principal support for federal activities. During the Civil War, the financial needs of the Union government called for new revenue sources. First in 1861, Congress passed a vague act committing the North to an income tax. As the national debt increased, editorial writers called for a tax, rather than borrowing, to finance the war. Congress passed a second, less-ambiguous tax act as a war measure and then a series of taxes, including income, excises, and tariffs, to finance the war, which was costing about $2 million a day at a time when the Confederate Navy was severely cutting customs receipts. In the debate on one tax proposal in 1864, the issue arose as to whether the tax should be progressive, with higher percentages paid by persons of higher income; proportional, with everyone paying the same percentage of income; or flat, with everyone paying the same dollar amount. When Republican Congressman Augustus Frank, a railroad director from New York, proposed a progressive tax, he was attacked by Congressman Thaddeus Stevens of Pennsylvania, who thought it was "a punishment of the rich man because he is rich." Senator Charles Sumner of Massachusetts, like Stevens an abolitionist leader, defended progressive taxes based on the theories of J. B. Say, the French economist, and Adam Smith, that a rich man should be taxed not only in proportion to his revenue but somewhat more because he was more able to pay. Persuaded by the argument, Congress passed a more-progressive bill, under which those with incomes of $500 to $5,000 paid 5 percent and those with $5,000 to $10,000, 7.5 percent. Deductions for federal, state, and local taxes, mortgage interest, and repairs and losses from the sale of land were included. The debates over the Civil War taxes did not elicit constitutional objections from members of Congress, who saw the financial crisis as interfering with the war effort. The legislation they passed gave some guidance concerning the sort of taxing system that might evolve if the income tax ever became a consistent policy in peace time.[4]

Once the Civil War ended, public sentiment demanded an immediate repeal of the taxes. On March 15, 1872, Senator John Sherman stated the case:

> The public mind is not yet prepared to apply the only key to a genuine revenue reform. A few years of further experience will convince the body of our people that a system of national taxes which rests the whole burden of taxation on consumption and not one cent on property or income is intrinsically unjust. . . . Everyone must see that the consumption of the rich could not bear the same relationship to the consumption of the poor as the income of one does to the wages of the other.[5]

Reflecting the views expressed by Sherman, Congress permitted the entire series of existing income taxes to expire in the aftermath of the war, not to be revived until the Sixteenth Amendment. One of the measures enacted during the Civil War, a tax on lawyers' professional earnings, was challenged in the courts as a direct tax which could not be exacted unless it was apportioned among the states. In 1881, the Supreme Court decided in *Springer* v. *U.S.* that it was not a direct tax and therefore Congress could levy it under its general taxing powers without apportionment.[6]

In the period after the Civil War, Congress still relied primarily on import duties or tariffs and excises for raising federal revenue. But as the country rapidly industrialized, newer forms of wealth, such as stocks and bonds, which represented intangible property of banks, corporations, and private individuals, became significant as possible revenue sources. Farmers and agrarian radicals increasingly attacked the existing tax structure as unfair. They complained that relying on the tariff on imports as the major source of federal tax receipts required them to pay higher prices for manufactured goods in industries protected from competition from abroad, while they received low prices for the food they grew. They wanted an income tax and a revision of the tariff. As they gained influence, the Democratic party began gradually to favor a lower tariff and an income tax to make up the lost revenue.[7]

The income tax increasingly became a regional issue. Fourteen income tax bills were introduced into the Congress between 1873 and 1879 by congressmen from the Middle West and the South. Agrarian radical organizations, arguing the case of farmers harmed by low prices for their products and high tariffs on the goods they bought, continued to petition the Congress for an income tax and a lower tariff. Joseph Pulitzer, who became publisher of the *New York World* in 1883, instituted a long editorial campaign for an income tax in the cause of the poor, the forgotten man. Meanwhile, as the high tariff piled up higher surpluses in the Treasury, the Democratic party devoted itself to lowering the tariff. Henry George, the single taxer, preferred an income tax—taxing "men on what they have rather than what they need"—to a tariff, which taxed men on the necessities of life. In the prosperous 1880s when farm prices rose, the income tax movement subsided. But the 1890s saw prices decline again amidst the continued growth of large fortunes and trusts. Farmers complained repeatedly that the burden of general property taxation weighed more heavily on them while rich urban dwellers invested in securities and the wealthy business and professional classes escaped taxation. Complaints of the farmers about railroad rate abuses they experienced as they tried to move their goods to market were addressed in the Interstate Commerce Act of 1887. Congress also expressed an intention to deal with farmers' objections to the trusts in the Sherman Antitrust Act of 1890. However, in a period of economic exigencies either experienced or expected, those two actions did not dampen enthusiasm for an income tax.[8]

The Panic of 1893, a severe financial crisis and business depression resulting in decreased revenues from excises and imports, invigorated the income tax demands. Western Democrats led the way in insisting on such a tax, coupled with a small downward revision in the tariff. Congress responded by including in the Wilson-Gorman Tariff Act of August 15, 1894, a 2 percent tax on all income—rents, interests, dividends, salaries and profits—ungraduated as a flat tax on incomes above $4,000. Farmers were not pleased that the tariff rates were reduced only slightly, but they applauded the income tax measure. Business denounced the income tax as confiscatory and immediately cast about for a legal challenge to its validity. They found a vehicle in *Pollock* v. *Farmer's Loan and Trust Company*, a derivative suit attacking the new tax, brought by a stockholder against a company in which he owned shares. The tax could not be challenged directly by the corporation because an act of 1867 specifically banned suits for the purposes of restraining the assessment or collection of a tax "but not a refund after the tax is collected."[9]

Pollock was not really in opposition to the company, as they both wanted the tax declared illegal. But when he appealed from an adverse decision in the court below, the Supreme Court agreed to hear the case. The trust company hired an impressive battery of lawyers, including a former senator, to attack the measure's constitutionality. They submitted a large and impressive brief laden with history, law, and economic theory. The briefs argued three major points. First, the provision taxed income from land, which had historically been regarded as a direct tax. Because under the Constitution, direct taxes had to be apportioned among the states according to population, and there was no apportionment included in the legislation, the tax was unconstitutional. Second, Pollock's lawyers argued that since the income tax exempted incomes below $4,000, it violated the constitutional requirement that taxes be uniform throughout the nation. Third, they argued that the law was invalid under the Tenth Amendment to the Constitution, as an infringement of the reserved powers of the states. It attacked one of the most important state powers, control over its own revenue-producing instruments, including the income from state and municipal banks.[10]

One of the trust company's lawyers, former Senator George Edmunds of Vermont, argued that a system of income taxation would result in the richest people bearing the burden of taxation and the majority paying nothing. This policy he saw as leading to "Communism, anarchy, and then, the ever-following despotism." Edmund's fears arose in a period of agrarian radicalism, populism, a series of bitter strikes, and Coxey's Army marching on Washington, which some regarded as threats to the capitalist foundations of the country. The pleas of the company's lawyers found a receptive ear in the Court. The justices proceeded to distinguish the earlier carriage tax and lawyers' professional earnings cases as narrowly decided. Essentially, the Court in a 6-2 opinion held that the part of the law taxing income from land was an illegal direct tax on land itself. On the issue of whether, therefore, all parts of the law covering any income was unconstitutional, the Court was divided 4–4, one justice not participating because of illness. The decision in the lower court therefore stood, in part, and an income tax on anything other than state bonds and land remained valid.[11]

The lawyers for the company asked for and were granted a rehearing upon the ill justice's recovery. This time, voting 5–4, the Court declared that since parts of the law were unconstitutional, the entire law was defective. No income tax could be collected. In announcing the decision, however, the Court did not clarify the issue of what constituted direct taxes. Chief Justice Fuller's opinion stated that he could see no difference between income from land and income from any other property. If taxes on land were direct taxes, did this mean other income taxes were? If so, which taxes? The Court did not answer. As an interesting aside, the ill justice voted with the four in the minority, which means one of the four in favor of income taxes in the first case switched his vote. Historians have spent a great deal of effort on the subject, but still have not identified the justice involved.[12]

Joseph Pulitzer of the *New York World* pessimistically responded to the decision by declaring that the issue of the income tax was dead, although he believed the principle should remain alive. But those who believed a federal income tax was absolutely essential to reach the intangible forms of wealth created by the industrial revolution and to redress what they regarded as inequities in paying for the functions of the national government, did not abandon the struggle. They pointed out that other countries had income taxes. France had had one since 1793, and the British had reenacted an income tax in 1842, which soon became permanent and then progressive in 1910. However, when supporters tried to gain enactment of an income tax to finance the Spanish-American War, they failed.[13]

Over ten years had passed since the *Pollock* case, and still there was no income tax. The continuing quest began to appear futile. But in 1906, Republican President Theodore Roosevelt, speaking while laying the cornerstone of the House Office Building, surprised his party by suddenly interjecting a statement supporting an income tax. He projected the

> adoption of some such scheme as that of a progressive tax on all fortunes beyond a certain amount either given in life or devised or bequeathed upon death to any individual—a tax so framed as to put it out of the power of the owner of one of these enormous fortunes to hand on more than a certain amount to any one individual; the tax, of course, to be imposed by a national and not the state government.

All in one fell swoop, Roosevelt had promoted not just an income tax, but a progressive one at that. Supporters of the tax were jubilant. Businessmen, especially those in the President's own party who opposed a tax, were furious.[14]

But Roosevelt in his presidential message of December 3, 1906, repeated his call for an income tax, although warning of the difficulties in view of the *Pollock* decision without a constitutional amendment. In words reminiscent of Senator John W. Sherman in 1872, he stated, "The man of great wealth owes a peculiar obligation to the state because he derives special advantages from the mere existence of government." This obligation should "be recognized by the way he pays for the protection the states give him." But he warned, "it is quite as necessary that in this kind of taxation, where the men who vote the tax pay but little of it, there should be clear recognition of the danger of inaugurating any such system, save in a spirit of entire justice and moderation." By June 1907, Roosevelt advanced to the point of saying that "most great civilized countries have an income tax and an inheritance tax. In my judgment both should be part of our system of Federal taxation." But despite his rhetoric, Roosevelt actually did little to obtain an income tax.[15]

A series of Democratic defeats in successive presidential elections and the influence of big business interests in the Republican party meant that high tariffs persisted and an income tax seemed less likely. But supporters of the tax never gave up propounding the inequity of leaving so much national income free of what they characterized as a fair share of supporting the government's revenue needs. As Progressives in both parties became stronger in each session of Congress after 1905, they repeatedly proposed income tax bills. In 1908, the Democratic platform supported the idea, and William Howard Taft, the Republican candidate, approved the tax "in principle."[16]

When President Taft called the Congress into special session in March 1907 to fulfil a campaign promise to revise the tariff, Senator Joseph W. Bailey of Texas added an income tax proposal excluding state, county, and municipal bonds. He thought the *Pollock* cases had been wrongly decided and believed the exclusions in his amendment provided a sufficient basis to ask the Court to reconsider its decisions. Senator A. B. Cummins of Iowa modified Bailey's proposal for a flat tax on income above $5,000 to require a graduated tax running up to 6 percent on incomes over $100,000. When it became clear that Congress would approve some income tax levy, the Republican floor leader, Senator Nelson W. Aldrich of Rhode Island, introduced an alternative to levy a 2 percent excise tax on corporations. What he really wanted was to defeat the idea of an income tax. Aldrich adamantly opposed an income tax because, among other reasons, it would undermine support based on revenue needs for a high protective tariff on manufacturers, which he favored. He therefore worked out a compromise with Taft to support a corporation tax instead. Taft liked this suggestion because the Supreme Court had not addressed the validity of a corporation tax in *Pollock*. He did not want to be in the position of trying to undermine the Court's role as interpreter of the Constitution by legislative enactment. But when this strategy seemed doomed to failure after a counting of votes, Aldrich and other members of the Senate Finance Committee, in conferring with President Taft, decided to support the passage of a constitutional amendment.[17]

Even as the income tax amendment was voted out 77–0 in the Senate and 318–4 in the House, Aldrich and his adherents, as well as the Progressive supporters of the tax, thought it would never be ratified. The debate in the House, in which Republican proponents denounced the tax as too burdensome to those who were the most productive people in the society, made clear that their real objections to it were more than constitutional. Even though the Progressives knew the whole purpose was to kill the idea, they could not vote against a constitutional amendment directed at their objective of an income tax. As a last ditch, the Progressives tried but failed to get ratification by conventions rather than by state legislatures. They believed the entrenched power of business interests in state legislatures would prevent ratification. In conventions called expressly for the purpose of considering the amendment, they might stand a better chance. But contrary to predictions, the amendment was ratified by one state after another and became effective on February 25, 1913. Progressives, who feared the amendment might not be ratified, did not note that although two out of five Americans lived in the large cities in which business held sway, rural America still controlled legislatures in most of the states. Because farmers and rural interests were major forces behind the tax, Progressives did not need to fear the lack of state conventions or that the legislatures would not ratify. In addition, people in some states had long experience with an income tax since the day of the faculty tax and had not concluded it was objectionable.[18]

In some ways adoption of the Sixteenth Amendment had as far-reaching an import as the ratification of the Civil War amendments. The income tax became the most important source of federal finance. It helped to fund World War I, and it made it possible for the government to enact programs perceived as necessary from an assured source of revenue. Federal grants-in-aid and the whole panoply of social programs enacted during the New Deal and after, would have been impossible without it. It did partially shift the burden of federal finance to the wealthy, but only temporarily until their lawyers and lobbyists figured out ways to riddle the income tax code with shelters and deductions. The net effect, however, was to shift the burden from the lowest income people to the middle class. Eventually, dissatisfaction with the tax became obvious because of a general recognition that the progressive income tax has not been as progressive as its proponents thought. These objections, however, were coupled with satisfaction with the programs funded and an acknowledgment that paying taxes, as Oliver Wendell Holmes, Jr., pointed out, is "what we pay for civilized society."[19]

The income tax amendment succeeded ultimately because of several factors. The supporters did not lose heart and abandon the effort because of repeated failures. Intense, deep social discontent with the tariff mobilized agrarian radicals, populist politicians, and then Democrats and Republicans from agrarian states to agitate persistently for its enactment. Progressives gradually increased in number within the Republican party. When the issue seemed about to divide the Republicans irreparably, facing the power of public opinion reflected in congressional support, the party's leaders had to find a way to heal the breach even though they did not want an income tax. Some members of Congress, led by Congressman Cordell Hull of Tennessee, continued from 1907 to discuss the subject on the floor and to cite examples of its successes elsewhere in order to educate their colleagues. They understood that substantive amendment making is a long, drawn-out affair and did not lose heart. The Republicans outsmarted themselves by supporting a constitutional amendment because they thought it would never be ratified. They neglected to assess carefully existing state support for approval. The Progressives acted on principle, accepting a legislative compromise on the basis of hopes, while not being fully aware that they were really taking no great risk at all. The central problem was gaining enough consensus in the Congress. Even though one does not have to be a farmer to represent farm interests, perhaps the fact that no farmer was elected to Congress between 1892 and 1913 was a factor. Although neither side apparently knew it, the consensus for ratification already existed in the states. Only four states rejected the amendment: Connecticut, Florida, Rhode Island, and Utah. Pennsylvania and Virginia did not act. Instead of derailing the income tax amendment, the Supreme Court's negative decision in the *Pollock* case gave impetus to the move to gain an amendment rather than making an income tax impossible for all time.[20]

The redistribution of income the Progressives expected did not really happen. They might have been astonished at the quickly developing loopholes, which really are consciously legislated provisions enacted by the people's representatives. But probably they would also understand that tax policy has always been balanced between a need to raise revenue and a fundamental devotion to the free enterprise system. The Congress has consistently considered what tax breaks are needed—whether capital gains treatment, depreciation, or shelters—to keep productive entrepreneurs producing and profit seekers investing, while simultaneously desiring to equalize the burden of raising revenue for defense as well as for social programs.[21]

The income tax system has become increasingly unpopular with Americans even though they continue to want the "civilized society" taxes buy. Debates over loopholes, progressivism, or a flat tax continue today as they have since 1913. From a high of 94 percent in 1944–45, the top income tax rate was cut to 91 percent after World War II, to 70 percent in the 1964 Kennedy tax cut, and to 50 percent in the Reagan sponsored 1981 act. The tax rate at the lowest income bracket has fallen from 23 percent in 1944–45 to 11 percent in 1983. However, it has proved to be a constant source of revenue and a useful instrument for achieving desired social objectives and regulating the economy.[22]

The achievement of the income tax amendment offered another example of the need for amendment supporters to engage in a sustained struggle without pessimism. It also demonstrated that open, extended public debate on a matter of such consequence can help to build consensus even when it appears that the efforts are failing. State consensus, however, already existed, based on an awareness that something pernicious was happening that was unfair to farmers and other affected workers. This, combined with federal revenue needs, gave the unfairness issue deep poignancy. The Supreme Court's hostility toward doing something about the tax inequity served to deepen the proponents' resentment. Consistent with the Civil War amendments and income tax experiences, the fewer favorable decisions announced by the Supreme Court on a controversial issue of fairness and justice, the more likely resentment will build toward the necessity for amending the Constitution.

Controversial amendment supporters can also learn from the example of the Sixteenth Amendment the effectiveness of gaining consensus in enough states before pursuing congressional enactment of a proposal. Indeed, if the Sixteenth Amendment example were followed, supporters would delay enactment of an amendment by Congress until they were assured of enough votes in enough legislatures to gain ratification. As they gather enough state legislative votes, they should continue to express pessimism about ratification. In this way some congressional opponents might vote for passage believing the amendment would not be ratified. This might be a less-effective national organizing strategy, but it could prove more successful.

Generating an Artificial Consensus: Prohibition and Its Repeal

3

Prohibition amendment supporters succeeded in meeting the constitutional requirements for ratification in 1919, after a struggle as lengthy as that endured by abolition and income tax proponents. They organized effectively to convey a majority voter perception to enough congressmen and legislators that selling or making alcoholic beverages was a problem which could not be solved without changing the Constitution. But the consensus they generated was artificial. It was constructed from support for symbolic negative language, recognizing the major problem of alcohol abuse and opposing the free availability of alcoholic beverages and not from a desire to achieve the actual outlawing of drinking. Lack of enforcement and repeal in a few short years flowed directly from the absence of original agreement about its necessity. Just as war had provided the context for the achievement of the thirteenth, fourteenth, and fifteenth amendments, the false consensus generated for the Eighteenth Amendment was strengthened by the stress of World War I. When the war ended, the absence of consensus became starkly apparent. Due to this and subsequent events, the amendment was repealed.[1]

Prohibition evolved from the growth of the temperance movement, which had begun with the religious revivalism of the early nineteenth century and continued to be promoted by various churches. In 1811, the Presbyterian church denounced the sinfulness of drunkenness, and Methodist preachers were forbidden to sell spiritous liquors. Congregationalists in Massachusetts organized the Society for the Suppression of Intemperance in 1813. Moderation in drinking, not prohibition, was the most-often stated goal; however, the goal soon became outright abstinence. In 1825 reformist clergyman Lyman Beecher gave a series of widely publicized sermons on the need for temperance. In response, the American Society for the Promotion of Temperance was founded in Boston in 1826. Interest in the move-

21

ment waxed and waned nationally, led by the Washington Temperance Society in the 1830's, but by 1841 numerous persons who had been drinkers had taken the society's abstinence pledge. In this period, advocates usually argued that temperance was needed to prevent the progressive ruin of the family through the use of strong drink. They succeeded in tightening liquor laws in many states and stimulated outright prohibition of the sale of liquor in others.[2]

After the Civil War, reformers from the abolitionist and early temperance movements turned their attention again to the issue of "Demon Rum." When neither of the major political parties adopted the issue, the reformers founded the Prohibition party in 1869. In 1872 the party's presidential candidate received no more than 5,000 votes out of six million cast; however, by 1884 liquor was a significant issue in the campaign. The mother of the Republican candidate, James G. Blaine, had been an Irish Catholic, and his supporters particularly cultivated the Irish-American vote in New York state. Six days before the election, a delegation of Protestant clergymen met with Blaine at his New York hotel. Their spokesman called the Democrats "the party whose antecedents had been rum, Romanism, and rebellion." Blaine did not immediately reject this remark, which was widely publicized as a slur on the faith of Irish-Catholics as well as their drinking habits. Cleveland won the election by a narrow margin with the voting results in New York state proving decisive. Blaine's reputation for corrupt political behavior probably helped to defeat him, but the Republicans lost New York state by 1,047 votes when the Prohibition party candidate gained 24,999 votes, which could have gone to Blaine. Cleveland got the "wet" immigrant vote, while the Prohibition party, instead of Blaine, benefited from the "drys."[3]

In an annex to their 1888 platform, the Republicans opposed alcohol abuse, acknowledging that this was an issue in rural areas in which they had great strength. The party, they asserted, "cordially sympathizes with all wise and well-directed efforts for the promotion of temperance and morality." In the election, although Cleveland won a majority of 91,000 in the popular vote, Benjamin Harrison narrowly defeated him by a plurality of sixty-five electoral votes. However, the Republican platform was apparently not strong enough medicine for opponents of drinking as again the Prohibition party drained off 250,000 votes. After the rise of the Populists in 1892, successful presidential aspirants began to gain increasing majorities, and the Anti-Saloon League was organized. As a result of both these developments, the Prohibition party's power to influence election results was eclipsed.[4]

In 1896 the Anti-Saloon League, founded in Oberlin, Ohio, and led by Hiram Price, a long-time Republican congressman from Ohio, rose to challenge the Prohibition party. The League's practical political program gave support to "dry" candidates no matter what their views were on other issues. They did not care if the candidates drank, so long as they voted dry. The League was enormously successful in electing candidates in Ohio, its home base, and in making large parts of the state dry by local and county option. The "Ohio idea" they developed of using paid professional officials and workers—who gave their entire time to League activity—monthly subscriptions from members, and focusing on the single issue of liquor worked, and spread elsewhere. The League produced and disseminated voluminous literature, including advice on legislative lobbying, and it supplied detectives for dry communities to identify liquor law violators. Although the League was successful in rural areas, the large wet votes of Cleveland and Cincinnati kept Ohio largely wet until 1918. By another referendum in 1919, the people of the state disapproved the ratification of the Eighteenth Amendment by their rural-dominated state legislature, but to no avail. Only with the passage of the Nineteenth Amendment giving suffrage to women did a real popular voting majority for Prohibition emerge in the state.[5]

Prohibition on a national level began to play a major role in elections because of the activities of the drys. In 1913 in California, Nevada, Illinois, New Hampshire, New Jersey, New York, Rhode Island, and Wisconsin, both parties opposed Prohibition; in the Deep South, both parties supported it. In Colorado, the Republicans were dry and the Democrats were wet. In Oklahoma, the Democrats were dry and the Republicans were wet. In Indiana, the Republicans supported county option, while the Democrats supported local option. In Pennsylvania, both parties supported local option. Within the states, urban areas usually supported the wets and the rural areas supported the drys. This made all the more important the refusal of Congress, after the 1910 census, to give more seats to the cities in the House of Representatives, thus postponing reapportionment to 1930.[6]

The gathering strength of the Prohibition movement in the 1900s resulted, in part, from the alliances between the Progressive movement, the dry crusade, and the crusade for woman suffrage. Reformers who wished to end corrupt practices in government and the liquor trade, and to gain suffrage for women coordinated forces. The Progressives wanted to reform the urban political machines. They saw the saloon as a place where urban bosses gathered their troops of urban workers and recent citizens of immigrant descent, to march off to vote as they were told. The working men may have emphasized the role of the saloon as a good, well-lit, decent place to socialize for those who had little money or power; but the Anti-Salooners saw the city as evil and the saloon as a place of degradation. The drys supported the Progressives' reforms, and they in turn supported the drys.[7]

Women had been major supporters of temperance and had shown little dissatisfaction with their role in the moral suasion phase of the temperance movement that pre-dated the Civil War. When the movement began trying to gain prohibitionist legislation in the late 1840s, women began to feel, increasingly, their powerlessness in spurring legislative changes because they did not have the right to vote. Many temperance activists began to identify with support of women's rights. Susan B. Anthony, for example, showed little interest in women's rights at all until, as a delegate to the New York Sons of Temperance meeting in 1852, she was prevented from speaking because it was considered an inappropriate role for a woman.[8]

Women began to engage in vigilante activities—closing saloons in the 1850s—usually without being convicted by sympathetic male juries who regarded their efforts as devoted to maintaining the purity of the home and family. Interrupted by the Civil War, the demonstrations of 1873 when women prayed and begged saloons to close were reflective of the earlier movement. Temperance bills began to be introduced in the Congress, and the formation of the Women's Christian Temperance Union (WCTU) in 1874, which soon became the largest women's organization in nineteenth-century America, was an outgrowth of the movement. By the time Frances Willard became its president in 1879 for an eighteen year period, the Temperance Union was a tightly organized society that came gradually to support prohibition and woman suffrage. Because so many women reformers supported Prohibition, men who wanted it supported suffrage, assuming that women would vote for Prohibition. The Anti-Saloon League was founded in 1896, and soon supported woman suffrage for the same reason, to obtain more voters for the dry cause. The connection between woman suffrage and Prohibition seemed reinforced by the fact that of the eleven states (all in the West) which adopted female suffrage before 1917, seven were dry and the other four had areas of local option. Even though some feminists thought women might have been enfranchised earlier if Prohibition had not divided the wets and drys, suffragists became closely tied to the drys.[9]

The South had particular problems, but largely supported the dry cause. Some white southerners explained that they supported Prohibition first to keep liquor away from Negro males whose carnal lusts were stimulated by it and then from white males, who although less animalistic, could be driven eventually to degeneracy by its use. But their purist conception of womanhood and their desire not to exacerbate the issue of keeping blacks out of politics made them want to keep women out of the political arena. They believed the violence and intimidation used to disenfranchise black men could not be so blatantly used against black women.

In the election of 1916, the drys supported the policy of the Anti-Saloon League, voting for candidates with League backing. Alice Paul, head of the National Woman's party, attempted, unsuccessfully, to organize a protest vote against Democratic candidate Woodrow Wilson in the western states where women had the vote because he did not support woman suffrage. Republican candidate Charles Evans Hughes refused to take a pro-dry, pro-woman stand or a stand for any progressive cause, so neither drys nor women's rightists in the West could vote for him. The strains in the coalition were evident.[10]

The Prohibitionists used every organizing tactic possible to threaten candidates who refused to vote dry, to shape public opinion, and to elect candidates who would vote dry, no matter what else their voting records. The tactics proponents used had been initiated by the WCTU. The Anti-Saloon League adopted the lobbying techniques of the WCTU and refined them, adding the power of the evangelical churches. These included buttonholing representatives, preparing materials which could be inserted whole in newspapers, organizing petitions, packing legislative galleries with members, and sending an avalanche of letters to legislators. They also insisted on temperance education in the schools and mobilized children to march and sing at polling booths to denounce wets when local and county option elections were held. They organized telegram campaigns to flood the wires with messages before crucial votes. They would then inform constituents of how their representatives had voted.[11]

For the pamphlets, newspapers, and other materials the drys disseminated, they had sufficient grist from the mills of the educators, scientists, and doctors. They collected medical research on animals and humans and disseminated it as facts about the evils of alcohol in causing myriad diseases. By 1902 they succeeded in having every state except Arizona require temperance teaching in the schools. They also succeeded, by 1906, in having the publishers of over forty endorsed school texts include the doctrine that alcohol was poison. In three states, Iowa, Kansas, and Maine, Prohibition was on the books by 1905. Between 1906 and 1912, seven states enacted Prohibition laws. By 1919, before the enactment of national Prohibition, nineteen more states had passed Prohibition laws.[12]

Even with the tremendous barrage of temperance and prohibition activity, the drys did not succeed in outlawing liquor altogether. They worked to translate temperance into Prohibition, refusing all arguments that limited use of alcohol was not harmful. When World War I began, the Prohibitionists decided to gain a final national victory by arguing that Prohibition was necessary for military reasons. Patriotism and winning the war were the objectives. They argued that drinking beer was pro-German, and making alcoholic beverages unnecessarily used grain and foodstuffs that were needed for the war. In addition, they asserted that servicemen would be ineffective warriors if they drank. Centralization required by the war effort disposed of any complaints about states' rights. The need for food conservation, and transportation space to carry food, rather than beer, wine, or liquor, as well as military preparedness provided persuasive rationales.[13]

The Anti-Saloon League made it clear that they were using the war to finally achieve national Prohibition. The League Journal, *The American Issue*, of May 4, 1919 summed it up:

> The spirit of service and self-sacrifice exemplified in an efficient and loyal staff made it possible to take advantage of the war situation, and of the confusion which He whom we serve has wrought among our enemies.[14]

The first national legislative victory for the drys was the Webb-Kenyon Act of 1913 which forbade sending liquor into dry states. It was passed over President Taft's veto by a vote of 63–21 in the Senate and 246–95 in the House. All but two senators of the dry majority came from the South and West.[15]

On December 22, 1914, Congressman Richard Pearson Hobson of Alabama introduced a Prohibition amendment into Congress. Hobson was one of the best-known orators on the subject of race degeneracy through alcohol. A hero of the Spanish-American War, he was elected congressman from Alabama, and lectured forty or fifty weeks a year for the Anti-Saloon league, earning $71,250 in nine years. He argued, in part, when introducing the amendment that "liquor will actually make a brute out of a Negro, causing him to commit unnatural crimes. The effect is the same on the white man, though the white man being further evolved, it takes longer time to reduce him to the same level." Congressman Lindquist of Michigan focused instead on patriotism. Guns were not the only things that could destroy a nation. Alcohol would rob the nation of its manhood and strength. The wets tried to argue rationally that temperate use of alcohol was not evil, but failed. The resolution passed 197–190. Not enough for a two-thirds majority required for a constitutional amendment, but clearly the tide was turning. In December 1917, Congress passed the amendment after the United States had entered the war.[16]

In addition, Congress passed a law excluding liquor advertising from the mails, and banning the liquor trade—but not the use of liquor—in the District of Columbia; and a clause in the Food Control Bill of 1917 prohibited the manufacture of liquor in the United States until after June 30, 1919, unless demobilization was completed before that date. The Anti-Saloon League deliberately did not propose outlawing the use of liquor. They thought even dry members of Congress would not vote for denying absolutely the right of their wet colleagues to drink, no matter what threats they used. Therefore, the proposed Eighteenth Amendment outlawed only the manufacture, sale, or transportation of intoxicating liquors. The wets argued that the amendment was an invasion of privacy and personal liberty, but to no avail. Appeals to loyalty and patriotism, added to medical "facts" about the evils of liquor consumption were enough. The vote in the House on the Eighteenth Amendment was 282–128. Geography more than anything else dictated the results, and rural areas were over-represented in the House of Representatives. House members who voted for the resolution were largely from small towns and country areas. Most of the opponents were from large cities. In San Francisco, St. Louis, St. Paul, Chicago, Cincinnati, Cleveland, Detroit, and Boston, Prohibition laws were rejected during the period of consideration of the Eighteenth Amendment. In the Senate, of the twenty senators who opposed the amendment, nine came from the Atlantic states, seven from the South, who voted the principle of states' rights, and four from states where beer or wine interests would be injured by the amendment.[17]

Ratification was comparatively easy since twenty-seven states already had Prohibition laws, and it was to be done by state legislatures. Gaining a simple majority vote in each house in three-fourths of the states would not be difficult. The predominance of rural interests guaranteed the results. The necessary thirty-six states ratified in fourteen months, and only Connecticut and Rhode Island never ratified. Dating from the founding of the temperance movement in 1811, ratification took 108 years. Dating from the founding of the Prohibition party in 1864, it took fifty years.[18]

Rhode Island, a non-ratifying state, challenged the legality of the amendment in the Supreme Court. In this, the first case challenging the legality of a constitutional amendment, the Court decided that if amendments are approved as provided for in the Constitution, they are legal. Essentially, the only unamendable part of the Constitution is the provision in the amendment article, Article V, that no state shall be deprived of equal suffrage in the Senate without its consent.[19]

As soon as Prohibition went into effect, in January 1920, problems occurred. The Volstead Act, designed to implement enforcement, was to be administered by the Internal Revenue Service. Penalties for bootlegging were to be fines, jail terms of up to five years, and the seizure of property used in transportation. The fact that alcohol could be used meant that the entire effort consisted of finding manufacturers and transporters, which was not at all easy. Rich people bought

stocks of liquor, bootleggers and crime ran riot, and deaths from
drinking industrial alcohol increased enormously. Patronizing speak-
easies and drinking because it was illegal became favorite means of
exhibiting social status and rebellion. Since many members of Congress drank, they were not concerned about providing strong effective
enforcement. When efficient federal agents put some respectable citizens in jail, public intolerance grew by leaps and bounds. After the
experience of the 1920s, the morality of Prohibition seemed ludicrous
by the time of the Depression.[20]

The existence of an unenforced Prohibition amendment shocked
some conservatives who feared the experience would erode confidence in maintaining law and order as a responsibility of constitutional
government. Their fears brought about the creation of an organized
movement against Prohibition. The Women's Organization for National Prohibition Reform led the fight to show that not all women
were drys—they just opposed intemperate consumption of alcoholic
beverages. Captain William H. Stayton organized an Association
Against the Prohibition Amendment, which came to include many
prominent conservatives, such as the Dupont brothers, as members.
Well funded and led by Executive Director Jouett Shouse, by 1929
the Association was very effective in lobbying for repeal.[21]

The efforts of the repeal organization bore fruit in the general
atmosphere of opposition to Prohibition. On February 16, 1933, the
Senate voted 63–23 to submit the Twenty-first Amendment to the
states. The House voted 289–121 to do the same. The North voted
wet, the Midwest voted half wet and half dry, Kansas and the Far
West voted dry, and the South and border states voted wet. On December 5, 1933, Utah became the thirty-sixth state to vote for the
Twenty-first Amendment. States could still be dry, and shipping liquor into a dry state was prohibited, but national Prohibition was ended
as ratification came easily. Repeal was assured by sending the amendment to the states to be voted on by conventions. Delegates were to
be chosen by a numerical majority so that geography would not prevail. The wets refused to opt for temperance—they went for repeal
of Prohibition, ignoring the evils of intemperate drinking.[22]

The drys lost, in part, because the wets used some of the same
arguments they had used, turned upside down. If the Eighteenth
Amendment sobered America to win the war, repeal would put drinking Americans to work to end the Depression. Racketeering, bootlegging, and immorality would be ended. Of course, Prohibition did not
win the war, and repeal did not end immorality. The wets also won
because they emphasized the threat to democratic institutions of having an amendment which was consciously unenforced, even though

it was part of the Constitution. In addition, the national treasury could use the funds generated by a tax on legal liquor.

The abstainers also lost because both the previously existing support in the states and the national consensus they had developed were based on support for nondrinking as a symbolic idea. Majorities could be gained to support the principle of nondrinking as a question of religion, morality, or efficiency. But majorities were unwilling to support the idea of actively forcing people who wanted to drink, not to drink. Prohibition advocates seemed to understand this and did not press for enforcement in the face of widespread violations of the law. But Prohibition did constrict drinking and legal employment in the industry until the Depression gave arguments for employment and tax revenues greater potency. The Depression also eroded cultural differences between rural farmers and urban workers, who both became more interested in jobs than in other issues.[23]

A national consensus for Prohibition was, in part, simulated by creating political fear among some congressmen by the exigencies of war. In addition, the delayed reapportionment of the House of Representatives gave the rural areas an advantage in the vote. There was no real consensus in three-fourths of the states to enforce Prohibition actively, but the movement's leaders took advantage of malapportioned legislatures and the symbolic nature of the proposal to gain ratification. By the Depression, the symbol was no longer as important as the reality of apparent economic necessity.

When the majority of the people spoke, as they did in the conventions called to ratify repeal, they responded by overturning the Prohibition amendment. Of the thirty-seven states that held state-wide referenda on the issue, in only five (North Carolina, Mississippi, Kansas, Oklahoma, and South Carolina) did a majority vote against repeal. It took less than a year for ratification, from February 1933 until December 5, 1933.

For supporters of other controversial proposed amendments, including ERA, the course of Prohibition amendment-making underscores the power of symbolism in gaining and losing consensus for constitutional change. It underscores as well the failure of symbolism as a basis for engendering actual change, even if ratification of a symbolic amendment is successful. When a broad interpretation was aggressively pushed after an amendment touted as only symbolic was adopted, it threatened the very existence of the amendment.

Gaining Woman Suffrage: The Nineteenth Amendment 4

In the struggle to gain consensus for a woman suffrage amendment, supporters had on their side a powerful tradition of representative government, based on the consent of the governed, as old as the Declaration of Independence and the founding of the Nation. But they were also opposing another powerful tradition in conflict with it, concerning appropriate roles for women. That tradition exhibited variations in different regions of the country, but it was essentially the view that, because women were intellectually inferior, morally superior, in need of protection, and dependent on men, they had no place in the disorderly world of politics. The potency of this tradition made demonstrating the necessity for woman suffrage a difficult matter. Furthermore, divisions among suffrage supporters over tactics and strategy helped to delay progress. As in the case of the income tax and the Fourteenth Amendment a negative Supreme Court decision helped to engender support. But proponents needed seventy-two years, from the first introduction of the proposal at Seneca Falls in 1848, to gain the consensus required for successful ratification of the Nineteenth Amendment.

Some women had the right to vote in the colonies, until colonial legislatures repealed it. New Jersey, in 1776, permitted women who were over age twenty-one, who had at least fifty pounds worth of property and who were at least one-year residents to vote. But the provision was repealed in 1806. The national Constitution of 1789 permitted participation in federal elections only by those who were permitted to vote in elections for "the most numerous branch" of each state's legislature. Therefore, so long as state laws did not extend the suffrage to women, they could not vote in federal elections. Some women continued to seek political rights, and, determined to gain more practical and legal control over their own lives, organized a strong movement in the late antebellum period.[1]

Women in the women's rights movement insisted on control over their own wages and property, joint guardianship over children, and improved inheritance rights when they were widowed. But the right to vote, the most controversial demand in the Seneca Falls Declaration of 1848 (drawn up by Elizabeth Cady Stanton, Lucretia Mott, and others, as the first public protest against the treatment of women as inferior), gradually gained a central place in the struggle. Although mostly relevant to the propertied classes, women had more success (through a series of married women's property acts) in the enactment of legislation to achieve their economic than political demands in the nineteenth century. By the time of Reconstruction, with the enactment of the franchise for freedmen, women still could not vote. Critics of woman suffrage, including many women, continued to believe that the public participation of women in politics on an equal basis would change woman's role as wife and mother, as well as her intellectual status, and would lead to demands for sexual equality in the home. Such a change, they asserted, would operate to the detriment of family stability and the welfare of children.[2]

The leaders of the women's rights movement were abolitionists and women's groups worked assiduously, through the National Women's Loyal League (organized by Elizabeth Cady Stanton and Susan B. Anthony), for a constitutional amendment outlawing slavery. In its incipient stages, the movement was greatly influenced by strategies and ideas developed in the anti-slavery struggle. Women could work for abolition as an expression of Christian charity, and religious work had long been accepted as an appropriate extension of the home for their sex. But once slavery was abolished in the Thirteenth Amendment, they began to focus more particularly on suffrage. They believed that when blacks gained the right of political participation, women would be included.

Many blacks asked for economic rights, including land for the freedmen, as a fundamental basis for assuring freedom and equality; but the most important black leader, Frederick Douglass, and his adherents preferred to emphasize political rights, which could be used to gain and protect economic opportunity. Suffragists were divided when it became clear that women would not be enfranchised along with black men. Black women such as Frances Ellen Harper, and white women such as Julia Ward Howe and Lucy Stone, were willing to delay suffrage for women and support suffrage for black men if they could not achieve both. Sojourner Truth took the opposite view, joining Stanton and Anthony in opposing suffrage for black men only. Some Republican political leaders saw black suffrage as a less controversial and expensive response to the freedmen than acceding to their demands for economic benefits. Furthermore, some party leaders believed black suffrage would be the linchpin that would ensure Republican party political power. Because of the urgency of insuring the enactment of black male suffrage, the Republicans did not want to jeopardize their efforts by proposing the more controversial idea of woman suffrage. Much to the consternation of some women's rightists, they were left out of the Fourteenth and Fifteenth amendments.[3]

Consequently, instead of seeing black suffrage as a real, yet unenforced response to black demands for equality—the quest for land having been rejected—some suffragists saw the exclusion of women's rights solely as an abandonment of their interests. Angered at the lack of Republican support, these women turned to some of the worst elements in the Democratic party for support. Anthony and Stanton joined forces with George Train, a wealthy anti-black Democrat who financed a newspaper for them, to appeal for the franchise for white women in order to counter the effect of black male voting, which, they claimed, could lead to black supremacy. Stanton, arguing against the Fifteenth Amendment, stated that it was wrong to elevate an ignorant and politically irresponsible class of men over the heads of women of wealth and culture, whose fitness for citizenship was obvious. She asserted, in behalf of a woman suffrage amendment

> If you do not wish the lower orders of Chinese, African, German, and Irish, with their low ideas of womanhood to make laws for you and your daughters . . . to dictate not only the civil, but moral codes by which you shall be governed, awake to the danger of your present position and demand that women, too, shall be represented in the government.

These appeals to prejudice by white women leaders were unfortunate. They undermined the moral force of their demand for suffrage, based on the highest purpose of broad representation in a political democracy. Furthermore, the posture taken helped to identify the women's movement as an upper middle-class white women's movement, and as essentially racist, although some black women ardently supported women's suffrage.[4]

Facing the exclusion of women from the Fourteenth and Fifteenth amendments, the suffragists needed a well organized campaign to achieve their objective. This was particularly the case since many women had to be persuaded that the idea would not prove detrimental to families by challenging women's traditional place in the home. But instead of reconciling their differences, they formed two separate organizations. The National Woman Suffrage Association, for women only, was organized with Stanton as its president in 1869; and the leaders of the New England Association (who supported suffrage for black men as a temporary expedient) formed the American Woman

Suffrage Association a few weeks later, with Republicans and abolitionists as major supporters, and Henry Ward Beecher as president. Both organizations were designed to achieve woman suffrage, but the Stanton group decided to include all women's rights issues, while the Beecher group focused only on the suffrage.[5]

Whatever contributions to a development of women's rights consciousness these organizations made, divided and fighting among themselves, they did not gain inclusion of women's suffrage in the Constitution. In 1866, Senator Edgar A. Cowen, Republican of Pennsylvania, had tried to amend a bill to give the vote to blacks in the District of Columbia, to provide woman suffrage, but failed by a 9–37 vote. In 1868, Republican Senator Samuel C. Pomeroy of Kansas presented a proposed suffrage bill to the Senate, and Indiana Congressman George W. Julian presented a joint resolution on the subject to both houses in 1869. Both proposals died without a vote being taken. Twelve resolutions to extend suffrage to women were introduced between 1875 and 1888 in the Congress. Usually they were reported back to the committee to which they had been referred, with extended reports from the majority and the minority. In 1878, Senator A. A. Sargent of California, a friend of Susan B. Anthony's, introduced into the Senate the Anthony amendment, which is the text of the Nineteenth Amendment as finally passed by Congress. After hearings, Sargent's proposal was reported adversely back to committee. In 1887, a women's suffrage amendment gained a vote on the Senate floor, but lost 34–16. Twenty-two of the opposing senators were from the South. In 1888, Mason of Illinois unsuccessfully attempted to give "widows and spinsters" the right to vote, on the rationale that they had no male voter to represent their interests.[6]

In the National Association, President Stanton's support of Victoria Woodhull, which she regarded as consistent with women's rights, did not help the movement. Woodhull, a charismatic, clairvoyant stockbroker and courtesan, and a vocal supporter of woman suffrage, appeared on the scene in 1871. She publicly avowed "free love," and made charges leading to a titillating scandal and lawsuit, alleging sexual misconduct against the first president of the American Suffrage Association, Henry Ward Beecher, and the wife of reform editor Theodore Tilton, both of whom were Beecher's parishioners. Although Beecher was acquitted, identification of the movement with the taint of immorality impeded further progress and further divided the two suffrage organizations.[7]

Gradually, however, age, maturity, judgment, persistent agitation, and organization enabled the suffragists to regain some lost ground. Anthony orchestrated helpful publicity from time to time. For example, arrested for voting, along with three of her sisters and twelve other Rochester women in the presidential election of 1872, she was found guilty and fined $100, which she never paid. The judge did not order her arrested because his Republican supporters did not want further publicity about the issue. In addition, he did not want her to be in a position to appeal the case to a higher court. The Grant administration quietly pardoned all sixteen women and the election inspectors who let them vote. In addition, her organization continued to hold national meetings every year in Washington, thus gaining some political support. The Anthony amendment was repeatedly introduced in Congress and reported out of committee until 1896, but consistently met failure.[8]

In the meantime, the Supreme Court made it clear that nothing but an amendment would give women the suffrage. Francis Minor, a St. Louis lawyer, sued for his wife's right to vote, based on the Fourteenth Amendment's clause that no state shall abridge the privileges and immunities of citizens of the United States. His wife was president of the Missouri Woman Suffrage Association. In 1875, the Supreme Court, in *Minor* v. *Happersett*, ruled that this clause did not apply to state laws preventing women from voting.[9]

Undaunted by the Court's decision, and with Stanton hoping it would help their argument that they needed a constitutional amendment, the two organizations continued the long weary battle of trying to gain the suffrage. The National Association focused on a federal constitutional amendment, while the American Association tried to gain suffrage state by state. But they made little progress in persuading the public that female voting was necessary, or that, in the alternative, denying the right was an egregious violation of democratic rights that needed remedying.[10]

In the late nineteenth century, the women's movement gradually began to recognize the need to heal its divisions before a major push for woman suffrage could be made throughout the country. The divisions did not seem to make much sense anyway. Suffragists outside the East, where the great battles over the Fourteenth and Fifteenth amendments had taken place, found the continued separation between the National and American Associations irrational. Little progress was being made on the issues relative to marriage, divorce and family in Stanton's agenda. There were more professional writers and women of independent means in the movement, and, during a period of social turmoil, of strikes and radical labor organizations, both organizations had become more focused on suffrage alone. In the absence of any basic disagreement, the daughter of Lucy Stone, Alice Stone Blackwell, and the leaders of the Women's Christian Temperance Union worked to bring the National and American Associations together.[11]

The merger was accomplished in 1890 with Stanton as president of the new organization, the National American Woman Suffrage Association. However, geographic schisms still emerged at every convention over strategy, tactics, and timing on such issues as whether to proceed state by state, or to go all-out for a federal amendment. Stanton also continued to stray from the suffrage-only focus; for example, when she published *The Woman's Bible* in 1895, a work with which the Association disavowed any connection. When Anthony succeeded Stanton after two years, she was better able to minimize the disputes. In 1900, Anthony chose as her successor Carrie Chapman Catt, who had been a very effective chairwoman of the Association's organization committee from 1895 to 1900. Catt served for four years, until, some historians believe, she was forced to resign by New Yorkers and southerners who objected to her support of Anthony's federal amendment after the organization had adopted a policy of proceeding state by state. Others cite her growing involvement in the international suffrage movement. Ann Shaw, who succeeded Catt but was not as good an organizer, let the state organizations follow their own instincts; the movement grew weaker. Southern women continued to argue that sectional and state prejudices had to be addressed, They believed that otherwise not enough state support to create a federal amendment could be generated. The Association acknowledged their point of view by announcing the principle of states' rights in the 1903 convention. State affiliates could use whatever approach they deemed necessary in campaigning for woman suffrage. This left southern members free to express their racism and northern members free to tolerate it, in a movement supposedly devoted to political rights for all.[12]

The consensus the suffrage supporters needed for their cause came faster in the West where a confluence of forces brought women the vote in Wyoming, Colorado, Utah, and Idaho. In Wyoming a peculiar combination of circumstances worked to achieve the first territorial adoption of woman suffrage in 1869. Esther Morris embraced suffragism at a lecture by Susan B. Anthony, which she attended after losing an inheritance because she was a female instead of a male heir. In South Pass, Wyoming, she began converting others to the cause of suffrage at private social occasions while preparing for the town's first election campaign. South Pass, the largest community in Wyoming, with 6,000 votes, had the largest number of women. Both candidates in South Pass endorsed woman suffrage, fearing the loss of some male votes through the influence of women. One of the candidates who was elected, whose wife was a suffragist, favored the idea and came to believe the cause was just. He thought she deserved the ballot since black males had been given the right to vote. His suffrage bill, introduced into the new legislature, passed. The governor of Wyoming, who was from Salem, Ohio (where he had attended a women's rights meeting) and was married to a suffragist, signed the bill into law. The legislature thought that giving women the vote would signal the kind of social stability that would attract good publicity and settlers to the new territory. By the time eastern antisuffragist arguments began to penetrate the area, it was too late to reopen the question. The result of female voting did little to change political events in Wyoming, despite the hopes of suffragists and the fears of antisuffragists. In addition, the peculiar circumstances of its passage in Wyoming could not be counted on to bring suffrage elsewhere. When Wyoming was admitted as a state in 1890, it was only after a heated debate in the Congress over whether admitting a suffrage state would encourage the granting of voting rights elsewhere. The Wyoming legislature prevailed when they made it clear that they would not give up women's suffrage as the price of admission to the Union.[13]

In Utah, where there were as many women as men, the elders of the Mormon church decided to give suffrage willingly to women. They believed the congressional criticism of polygamy in the territory would be deflected by letting women vote, who would thereby affirm their own belief in plural marriage. Therefore, women in Utah were given the vote in 1870. Stanton and Anthony welcomed the women into the National Association, but the American Suffrage Association rejected them because of their endorsement of polygamy. The Mormon strategy backfired when Congress, in 1877, reinforced the outlawing of polygamy, and took the vote away from Mormon women because of their complicity with the policy. But after Wyoming was admitted to the Union, with congressional acceptance of woman suffrage, the Mormon church gave up plural marriages, and in 1896 Utah was admitted to the Union, whereupon the state gave women the right to vote.[14]

While the Utah dispute was before the Congress, Colorado enacted suffrage. With the radical Populist party controlling the legislature, the state gave women the suffrage with male majority support in a referendum endorsing it. Historians have speculated about why Colorado acted as it did. Some assert that the difficult geography, climate and pioneer existence made the inhabitants radical in their approach to any issue. Others argue that the people in the many small towns, voting against the saloons and corporate interests, expected women to purify politics. Little, however, that could be called purification occurred.[15]

In 1896, Idaho, where populism also held sway during economic hard times, enacted woman suffrage. As a mass democratic movement, populism supported the extension of suffrage and women's participation in politics. Carrie Catt, who led the campaign in Colorado, was again at the forefront in Idaho. William Jennings Bryan carried the state in the 1896 election at which suffrage was enacted. At the same time, in Kansas, woman suffrage was rejected (according to Susan B. Anthony) because the Republicans and Whisky Democrats thought the women's vote would keep the state dry. The basis for this fear is unclear, because in none of the early four suffrage states did Prohibition become law before the Prohibition amendment. However, in California, the proliquor vote in the large cities did combine to defeat woman suffrage in 1896. For the next fourteen years, not one additional state gave women the vote, despite the organizational efforts of the National American Suffrage Association.[16]

Many of the women who were involved in the suffrage movement were prohibitionists, but the Prohibition issue could hurt or help the cause depending on local circumstances. The prohibitionist strategy of drying up the towns and rural areas by local options made the cities fear the women's vote, because many still believed women would vote dry. The Woman's Christian Temperance Union, founded in 1874 while the women's suffrage groups were divided, was extremely successful. It had many more members than the Associations. Frances Willard, the second president of the Temperance Union, was converted by Anthony and became an ardent suffragist, leading the organization gradually to support the suffrage efforts. Willard preached temperance, suffrage, and child labor protection, in the context of the acceptable female interest in strengthening the family. It was a "home protection" movement. After Willard's death in 1898, however, the Temperance Union reverted to focusing entirely on the dry cause.[17]

The dry cause continued to make faster progress than the suffrage movement, using local option and state laws. The South presented a special problem for the suffragists. The drys had great success there, but southerners did not permit black men to vote and were not about to endorse female voting with its implications for affecting the traditional role of women and its enfranchisement of black women. Women in the South worked for the drys in the interest of home and family, but did not mount a woman suffrage campaign. Some suffragists argued that the success of their cause was delayed by the liquor issue until after Prohibition was enacted. But the leading reformers in the Women's Christian Temperance Union who came from the upper middle class, gradually became more interested in suffrage than Prohibition. Being a suffragist became more fashionable than being involved in Prohibition activities, especially in the cities. By 1916, more women reformers belonged to the suffrage cause than to the Temperance Union. In fact, the controversy over liquor may have been beneficial, because many women had their first education as reformers in the Prohibition movement before moving on to the suffrage cause.[18]

After Stanton died in 1902 and Anthony in 1906, new leaders and issues came into prominence in the suffrage cause. Like Prohibition, progressivism helped the cause also. The emphasis in the Progressive movement on ending corrupt politics provided a reinforced rationale for including women voters, that is, as a means of purifying politics by insuring decisions that would protect the home and family. Women's clubs proliferated, and women's support for reforms (even when they could not vote) was a major force in the successes of the Progressive period. Their involvement helped to achieve enough support to enact woman suffrage in Washington, California, Oregon, Arizona, Nevada, Montana, and Kansas between 1910 and 1914.[19]

The votes for suffrage came from declining small towns, educated urban and suburban middle-class voters, and some of the working men in cities who saw the vote as a means for their wives and daughters to protect themselves. By the 1912 presidential election, two of the four candidates, Theodore Roosevelt and Eugene Debs, supported women's suffrage. Roosevelt, the Bull Moose candidate that year, had long supported feminist causes. His Harvard senior dissertation was entitled, "The Practicability of Equalizing Men and Women Before the Law." He did not publicly support suffrage, however, until he became the Progressive candidate on a platform supporting votes for women. Large numbers of women who could vote in some western states by 1912, voted for him, but they did not vote en bloc for his candidacy.[20]

New directions and new leaders emerged to advance the suffrage cause. The daughter of Elizabeth Stanton, Harriet Blatch, returned to New York after twenty years in England where she had experienced the militant suffrage tactics of the women there. She preached that the movement must broaden its base from the middle-class reformers and become more dramatically militant. She set up her own political union in 1907 to incorporate college students, factory workers, and union organizers. Then the wealthy Alva Belmont decided to give support to the suffrage cause on the condition that she be accorded power in it, offering the National American Association permanent headquarters in New York. But westerners and southerners did not welcome her involvement. When these women led their organizations to support their vice-president, Jane Addams, in endorsing Theodore Roosevelt in the 1912 election (even though the group was supposed to be non-partisan), Belmont withdrew her support. She joined the Congressional Union and its successor, the Woman's party, which she supported for many years.[21]

When Alice Paul and Lucy Burns, who had experienced incarceration and hunger strikes with British suffragettes, set up the Congressional Union in 1913 to focus solely on gaining a federal constitutional

amendment by more militant tactics, another strong element had to
be taken into account. Alice Paul had been named chairman of the
congressional committee of the National American Association at its
December 1912 convention. As committee chairman she organized a
suffrage parade of 5,000 women in March 1913, just before Woodrow
Wilson's inauguration. The women were mobbed and insulted, gen-
erating new publicity for the voting rights cause. Thereafter, she angered southerners by proposing that western Democratic women
voters be asked to vote Republican to frighten Wilson and the Democrats into voting a suffrage amendment out of Congress. She was
expelled for violating the National's bipartisanship policy, and for
being too assiduous in working for a federal amendment. She and
Burns established the Congressional Union and began attracting suffragists from the National. In 1917, Harriet Blatch's and Alice Paul's
organizations merged to form the National Woman's party, which
soon became very successful with its straightforward support of a
federal amendment.[22]

At this juncture, some women began to seek a states' rights constitutional amendment for woman suffrage. Kate Gordon, the Louisiana
president of the Southern States Woman Suffrage Conference, and
a member of the National Board of the National American Woman
Suffrage Association from 1901–1910, saw it as a way for the Democratic party to support women's rights. She began promoting the idea
in the early 1900's, repeating the now familiar arguments that en-
franchising white women was a way to maintain white supremacy in
the South. The proposal acknowledged that the South had moved
from violence and intimidation to more sophisticated means of preventing black men from voting. The states' rights amendment strategy
could permit southern states to grant suffrage to women, but to institute literacy tests and other procedural barriers used against black
men, to keep black women from voting. The approach failed to gain
broad support because, at about the same time, blacks started attacking
the procedural barriers as violations of the Fifteenth Amendment.
More importantly, many of the southern legislators had been using
states' rights arguments only as a smokescreen. Actually, they thought
voting for women was inappropriate. Furthermore, many northern
suffragists were committed to a national amendment approach as the
simplest strategy possible.

But the states' rights arguments did not go away. By 1914, some
leading suffragists persuaded the Association to support a substitute
amendment. Named for Democratic Senator John F. Shafroth of
Colorado and Congressman A. Mitchell Palmer of Pennsylvania, it
provided that if more than 8 percent of the legal voters in a state
petitioned for a referendum, and in the referendum a majority voting

on the issue voted favorably, women in the states could be enfranchised. The Association endorsed the proposal on the ground that congressmen would probably vote for it, even if they opposed suffrage, in order to give the local people a chance to express their wishes. Also, initiatives and referenda had become important progressive reforms accepted by both parties. In addition, as more states adopted suffrage they could be added to the list of those which would support the national Susan B. Anthony amendment. But almost as soon as the Association endorsed Shafroth-Palmer, a storm of opposition arose over the idea of conducting campaigns in each state for something less than the Anthony amendment, and the endorsement was dropped.[23]

Meanwhile, in 1915, Carrie Chapman Catt resumed the presidency of the National American Association. She increased membership from 100,000 to two million in two years. She cooperated with Alice Paul, but also kept up ties with Woodrow Wilson as she tried to get him to support women's suffrage. She was a seasoned political operator who understood that the militancy of the Woman's party offered a good counter pressure as she moved in a less threatening, more conciliatory fashion.[24]

In 1914, Alice Paul had tried to punish the Democrats for opposing suffrage by enlisting western women to vote against them in the midterm elections. She was not as successful as she had hoped, but when fewer Democrats than expected won, the Democrats in the House moved the suffrage amendment to the floor. However, the proposal was defeated, falling seventy-eight votes short of the two-thirds majority needed for passage.[25]

The election of 1916 tested the non-partisan policy of the National American Association against the Woman's party policy of supporting whatever party seemed more committed to suffrage. Because Wilson supported his party's platform of women's suffrage through state action instead of a national amendment, the Woman's party campaigned against him. Hughes ran on a Republican platform supporting a federal amendment, but Wilson won the election, although narrowly, with ten of the twelve states in which women could vote supporting him. As a result, members of Congress did not have to feel threatened by the female vote.[26]

In the face of such adversity, both the Association and the Woman's party renewed their efforts. By the time World War I was declared in 1917, antiwar sentiment had become a significant element within the women's reform movement, clouding the suffragists' efforts. Women reformers such as Jane Addams and Florence Kelley were confirmed pacifists. Carrie Chapman Catt was personally opposed to American intervention in the war because of her pacifism, but the

Association pledged support for the war effort. In fact, many women diverted their efforts from suffrage to war work, including joining the Red Cross and selling bonds. This patriotic posture helped in carrying New York state for suffrage in 1917, by dislodging the notion that women would vote for peace and not support the war. The suffrage cause was also helped by petitions, signed by over a million New York women asking for the vote, which disproved the notion that women did not want it. In the same year Rhode Island, Michigan, and Nebraska gave women the right to vote in presidential elections. By this time, a sufficient number of congressmen were from states in which women had the vote to generate enough consensus for passage in Congress of the Anthony amendment.[27]

During the war, women put on military uniforms, drilled, and worked in non-traditional occupations as streetcar conductors, mechanics, bricklayers, electricians, and armament factory workers. Wilson still hesitated to support a suffrage amendment, but Catt knew she needed him to get the southern states to ratify. She made it clear that she would leave him unpressured to determine when he would declare his endorsement. The National Woman's party, however, continued to picket the White House, heckled Wilson, and harassed the Senate. About a hundred women were arrested and went on a hunger strike, during which they were forcibly fed like the English suffragists, all with great publicity. Catt kept informing Wilson ahead of time about demonstrations, relying on him to value her confidence and to come around eventually to the cause. The Republicans in the House decided to embarrass the Democrats by supporting the amendment. It passed by just one vote beyond a two-thirds majority. Although Wilson then declared his support, the Democrats were still split, as mostly southerners voted against it. In the Senate, after the amendment failed by two votes to obtain two-thirds, Wilson asked the Senate to vote for it as a war measure, to make the world safe for democracy. But he still could not gain a sufficient number of Democratic votes.[28]

In 1918, the Republicans gained control of the incoming Congress in the off-year elections. The Association joined the Woman's party in campaigning against four anti-suffrage senators, two of whom were defeated. Seeing the handwriting on the wall, the Democratic leadership tried to pass the amendment in the lame duck session so as not to be blamed for its lack of success, but failed by one vote in the Senate. In the new Congress it passed in the House by a 3-1 voting margin, and in the Senate by two-thirds, with the South still in opposition. The southern Democrats voted negatively because they did not fear retribution at the polls; and they felt their constituents supported their efforts to keep black women, along with black men, from the polls, and to keep women out of the political arena. However, with the groundwork already laid in the states, ratification came rapidly. Northeastern state voters, fearful of adding immigrant women to those immigrant men whose vote they believed was influenced by political bosses, and the South with its traditional attitudes toward women, remained obdurate. All of the western states and most of the remaining northern ones ratified, until there were thirty-five. Finally, Tennessee ratified, bringing the number to thirty-six. During the ratification process, Catt insisted that women would not be the captives of any party. She cited the example of her work with Wilson and with the Republicans to gain suffrage. She asserted that she did not want women to be tied to one party, as blacks had been tied to the Republicans. Nor did she want them to alienate the Democrats. Once victory was won, Catt followed through on her assertions. She arranged to have the final victory convention of the Association become the first meeting of the non-partisan League of Women Voters.[29]

Unrelenting, though unsuccessful, the anti-suffrage American Constitutional League, in April 1920, began filing lawsuits to keep the amendment from going into effect. The Maryland League for State Defense challenged the amendment by bringing suit against the registration of two Baltimore women for the 1920 election. They argued that the constitutional guarantee, that no state's equal representation in the Senate would be changed without the state's consent, had been violated. They asserted that the basis of election of senators had been determined by thirty-six other states, without Maryland's consent, making the amendment illegal; but the Baltimore Court of Appeals dismissed the suit. Another suit, filed in the U.S. Supreme Court in 1921 by the same group and advancing similar claims, was also dismissed. Insulated from charges of illegality, it remained to be seen what women would do with their vote.[30]

One harbinger of future difficulties in the struggle for women's equality came from the identification of the suffrage cause as a white women's movement. When Susan B. Anthony asked ardent women's rights supporter Frederick Douglass not to speak at the Association's convention in 1894 in Atlanta, Georgia, for fear of offending southern sensibilities, she irritated large numbers of blacks. At the suffrage march organized by the National American Woman Suffrage Association and Alice Paul's Congressional Union in 1913 in Washington, the day before Wilson's inauguration, Ida Wells-Barnett, a black leader of the Illinois Alpha Suffrage Club, was told not to march with the Chicago contingent, but to stay at the rear so as not to disturb southern women. Wells-Barnett defied the leaders by stepping into line between two Chicago white women and proceeding along the line of march.[31]

These were only examples of a general pattern of insensitivity or

anti-black bias, whether for expediency or otherwise, on the part of
suffragist leaders. They achieved their objectives while exhibiting their
prejudices, but the Nineteenth Amendment meant suffrage largely
for white women until the Voting Rights Act of 1965 was passed. In
fact, the white supremacy arguments for woman suffrage had little
positive effect in the South. Most of the southern state legislatures
voted against ratification of the Nineteenth Amendment.[32]

The consensus required to gain the Nineteenth Amendment
evolved only with great difficulty. In the face of opposition or lukewarm support from many women, the movement's leaders abandoned
the strategy of emphasizing that women needed to act as individuals,
and that suffrage would make far-reaching changes in women's roles
in society. Instead, the reformers pointed to the lack of change in the
roles of women, men, and children in the western states in which
women could vote, and the continuing male economic control in the
society, as an argument to gain consensus. In doing so they effected
a reconciliation between two apparently conflicting traditions and undermined many of the arguments of suffrage opponents. They also
argued that expanding the suffrage to women would fulfill the American tradition of representative government without negative effects,
and with the positive influence of validating the existing political system. Because the amendment was largely self-enforcing, proponents
did not have to worry that if women voted to make substantive changes
in society they would face repeal as had the Prohibition supporters.
Once there were enough suffrage states to make female voters a significant factor in presidential elections, candidates for that office had
to take a position on the issue. Congressmen and senators in the suffrage states also had to pay attention to the women's desire for a
federal constitutional amendment. The attention paid to states' rights
and the race issue to placate the South was largely wasted.

Many southern state legislators simply opposed changing the traditional role of women to include political participation and used the
other issues as camouflage when dealing with suffragists. In the final
stages of the struggle, the militant and direct action tactics of the
National Woman's party gave additional credibility to the moderate
reform efforts of the Association. As in the case of the symbolic Prohibition amendment, state-based consensus helped to develop a national consensus, which was aided by the exigencies of war in which
women gave patriotic supportive services.

Judging from the history of the woman suffrage battle, gaining
effective state amendments to be used as a base from which to draw
states to ratify a controversial federal amendment would be a workable
strategy. Also, supporters could accept militant tactics, such as hunger

strikes and direct action, in an attempt to gain ratification, following Catt's example. They could draw attention to their less-militant behavior in the cause, while understanding that direct action carried out persistently over a long period of time can help to create the climate necessary for ratification.

Following ratification of the Nineteenth Amendment, as women's votes continued to be undifferentiated from men's, no immediate far-reaching changes occurred in women's roles. But in the 1920s women who had become suffragists in order to promote progressive social causes, and others who had focused on the vote as an end in itself, participated in a wide variety of causes, including maternal and child health, consumer legislation, making government more efficient and less corrupt, jury service, and conservation. They also became involved in the unsuccessful movement to gain a constitutional amendment to outlaw the use of child labor. Others in the National Woman's party transferred their single-issue focus, now that suffrage was gained, to an effort to gain an equal rights amendment.

Social Reform between the Wars: Losing the Child Labor Amendment

5

The history of the child labor amendment provides a striking example of how gaining consensus in the Congress does not mean similar consensus in enough states to achieve ratification. The child labor supporters seemed to learn little from earlier successful amendment supporters. They did not develop a strategy for ensuring enough state consensus before gaining congressional enactment of their proposals. They failed to prepare adequately for the dissemination of negative information during the ratification campaign. Also, they kept asking for the enactment of legislation to achieve their objectives, which betrayed their own confusion about whether they even needed a constitutional amendment to achieve their goals. Consequently, they failed to achieve a child labor amendment.

Women were very much a part of social reform movements in the 1920s and 1930s, of which child labor was only one aspect. Their involvement in these causes spurred their efforts in the struggle to gain the child labor amendment. By the 1920s, women's recent experience in the suffrage fight in Congress, in new employment opportunities and in home-front support activities in organized war relief efforts geared them for continued outside-the-home activities. Women had sold bonds, conserved food, manned war plants, and served as nurses. Following the war, reformers in the League of Women Voters and the Women's Joint Congressional Committee (WJCC) kept up their involvement in progressive causes. The Congressional Committee, especially, worked to expand appropriations for the Children's and Women's Bureaus and to gain the enactment of child labor laws and maternal and child health legislation. Although the National Woman's party focused on gaining an ERA in this period, some individual members aided social reform efforts.[1]

After a major report by the Children's Bureau on the subject of maternal and child health, in 1917, Julia Lathrop, chief of the Chil-

dren's Bureau since 1912, recommended a bill for federal aid to the
states to provide public health protection for maternity and infancy.
The bill was patterned after the Smith-Lever Act of 1914 which gave
matching funds to states for county agricultural extension agents.
Jeannette Rankin, elected as the first woman in Congress in 1916,
introduced the Maternal and Child Health bill in 1918, but President
Wilson did not encourage its passage. Senator Morris Sheppard (D,
Texas) and Congressman Horace Towner (R, Iowa) submitted the bill
again after women were enfranchised in 1920. The League of Women
Voters succeeded in gaining the approval of the Democratic and Republican parties, and Warren Harding supported the proposal in his
campaign. Female lobbying groups, such as the WJCC, made passage
of the bill their major legislative objective. After congressional enactment, President Harding signed the Sheppard-Towner Act on November 23, 1921. Jeannette Rankin was not re-elected after she voted
against United States entry into World War I in 1917, and the only
woman in Congress in 1921, anti-suffragist Alice Robertson of Oklahoma, voted against it. To the relief of women's reformers, she was
defeated in a re-election bid.[2]

Opponents continued to attack the maternal and child health program as a Communist measure designed to interfere with the family.
Also, medical groups, including the American Medical Association,
characterized it as governmental meddling with physicians by directly
providing certain services. However, the states implemented it
quickly; many women physicians and health care providers found
professional opportunities in its programs, and it survived a Supreme
Court test of its constitutionality in *Massachusetts* v. *Mellon* and *Frothingham* v. *Mellon* in 1923. The fight over the program continued in
appropriations hearings, but it survived until 1928, at which time it
lapsed as Herbert Hoover did nothing to help save it. The program
and services it funded were not revived until the New Deal. Antisuffragists, extreme conservatives (who denounced it as part of a
Bolshevist conspiracy), states' rights advocates, and the American
Medical Association joined in killing it.[3]

The opponents of Sheppard-Towner were also opponents of the
child labor amendment. The problem of child labor that the reformers
wanted remedied resulted from the rapid mechanization of production in the nation in the nineteenth century. The factory system
brought children into industrial jobs as wage earners. In the last decades of the nineteenth century, their numbers increased enormously.
By 1900 one child in six between the ages of ten and fifteen worked
for wages, amounting to more than 1,750,000 child laborers in the
country. Unlike the traditional apprenticeship system, child workers
became the prisoners of arduous, often dangerous work at long hours

in the routinized factory. By 1860 six states had limited child labor
to a ten-hour day in industry, and four states excluded the youngest
children under their police powers.[4]

Although laissez-faire economics, the profit motive, and social attitudes about the benefits of work delayed aggressive reform efforts,
by 1900 most states had enacted some form of legislation. But even
more importantly, a view of child labor as destructive began to take
hold. The old attitudes died hard, however, especially in the South.
The growth of cotton mills provided more opportunities for families
to increase their income by putting their children to work in the mills.
Various machine operations had long been executed by children in
the New England mills. Tending spindles, for example, soon became
so much a children's occupation, especially for those under ten years
of age, that by 1900 the southern mills employed more children than
any other sector of American industry.[5]

When the principal southern states did not enact child labor legislation as had other states, northern businessmen claimed that southern manufacturers had a price advantage which amounted to unfair
competition. In addition, muckrakers and other reformers publicized
incidents of extreme exploitation nationwide. As a result, even though
the South was not the only region to use child labor, it became a target
of the reform movement. Edgar Gardner Murphy, an Alabama min-
ister, took the lead in demanding state legislated controls and founded
a National Child Labor Committee on April 15, 1904. The dominant
influence in the group, concentrated in the major cities of the eastern
seaboard, consisted of social workers, educators, and philanthropists,
many of whom were female. The committee investigated and disseminated facts concerning child labor in order to arouse public and parental concern and to enact state, not national, legislation. It wanted
to keep children under age fourteen in school and out of work, and
to ensure that those between fourteen and sixteen were protected
from excessive hours and night work. The committee's efforts between
1904 and 1907 led two-thirds of the states to enact or strengthen
legislation. The South still resisted, insisting on protecting its peculiar
institution.[6]

Some public officials thought the federal government had a role to
play in regulating child labor. Senator Albert Beveridge, a popular
national figure since the Spanish-American War as a proponent of
overseas expansion and then a leader of progressive causes, made an
extended appeal for national legislation during three days of Senate
debate in January 1907. His presentation, replete with statistics and
data, described conditions not just in the South, but in Pennsylvania
coal mines, Ohio glass factories, and New Jersey sweatshops. He believed the national existence of the problem demanded a national

solution. Furthermore, he argued that recent Supreme Court decisions upholding the use of the commerce power to keep objectionable goods out of interstate commerce provided a constitutional basis for the enactment of a national law. His colleagues agreed with him about the need for some reform, but they were not yet ready to concede it should be national. Conservative senators rebutted his legal arguments by claiming that what he really wanted to do was to invade states' rights by controlling production, not commerce, in the states.[7]

Although Congress did not enact legislation, at President Roosevelt's behest, it did appropriate $150,000 for an official investigation of the condition of child and female labor in the country. The National Child Labor Committee had discussed Beveridge's bill with him and endorsed it, although Edgar Gardner Murphy and one group of trustees thought it unconstitutional and that it violated their central organizing principle of proceeding through state action. When Beveridge's bill died, the committee withdrew its endorsement and committed itself to waiting for the congressional investigation before taking an official position. Thereafter, however, the committee focused its efforts on securing state legislation and backing the establishment of a federal children's bureau.[8]

A setback occurred when the Supreme Court decided, in *Lochner* v. *New York* in 1905, that a state minimum hour law for bakers was unconstitutional. The case involved a New York law that regulated conditions of labor in the baking industry. The statute controlled safety, sanitation conditions, and hours of labor. In order to protect the workers from such hazards as excessive inhalation of flour dust, they could work no more than sixty hours a week or ten hours in any one day. The Court found that the law violated the freedom of workers to contract under the Fourteenth Amendment. As a result of the Court decision, state legislatures were warned against interfering with trades and occupations. But when, in *Muller* v. *Oregon*, that state's Ten Hour Law for women passed Supreme Court muster in 1908, new strength was gained for the regulatory movement. Florence Kelly, general secretary of the National Consumers League and a trustee of the National Child Labor Committee, encouraged the selection of Louis Brandeis as counsel and the use of a brief filled with descriptions of the harsh reality of industrial conditions. The case involved an Oregon law of 1903 that prohibited the employment of any female in any factory or laundry for more than ten hours a day. The Supreme Court upheld the law, distinguishing *Lochner* on the grounds that women's physical structure and biological functions made it reasonable for the legislature to provide special protection without a violation of the Fourteenth Amendment. When the Court upheld the law, and two years later the nineteen-volume federal report on women and child wage earners was distributed, a new period of state regulation of child labor ensued.[9]

By 1914, in the full tide of the Progressive movement and Woodrow Wilson's New Freedom, the National Child Labor Committee noted that forty-six of the forty-eight states had improved protective legislation or had provided for increased educational opportunities for children, although little actual implementation had occurred. Most progress had been made in ending the employment of children under fourteen. But not much had been done for those aged fourteen to sixteen. State legislatures seemed unwilling to make reforms that would put them at a competitive disadvantage with other industrial states.[10]

By 1914 the Supreme Court decided numerous cases upholding a national police power under both the tax and commerce clauses of the Constitution. In this setting the National Child Labor Committee changed its state-focused policy and decided to support national legislation. The committee looked at previous bills that had been introduced and, finding them defective, prepared its own bill. Their experts considered the commerce and tax powers as a basis for legislation and adopted Senator Beveridge's view that the commerce power could better withstand legal attacks. The bill they drafted prohibited the shipment in interstate commerce of products in whose manufacture children under age fourteen had been employed or children from fourteen to sixteen had worked more than eight hours in any day or forty-eight hours in any week. In hazardous jobs such as mining and quarrying, children under age sixteen were completely excluded.[11]

The National Child Labor Committee found two sponsors, A. Mitchell Palmer, a reform-minded Democrat from Pennsylvania, and Senator Robert L. Owen, also a Democrat and a Wilsonian progressive from Oklahoma. In testimony the organizations emphasized that the constitutionality of their approach was settled and spent little time in proving the evils of child labor which they believed had been well established previously. The bill passed the House 233–43, but thirty-five of the opposing forty-three votes came from six southern states. The Senate adjourned before action could be taken. But in the sixty-fourth Congress, Senator Owen and Congressman Edward Keating, Democrat from Colorado (who took the place of Palmer who had become attorney general), reintroduced the bill. The bill passed, again overwhelmingly, 337–46, on February 2, 1916. South Atlantic states principally voted against it. President Wilson took a hand in the proceedings by going to the President's Room at the Capitol to remind Democrats that support of a child labor bill was in their party platform. After his intervention, Republicans asked for immediate action in the

Senate. The Senate voted 52–12 to pass the bill on August 8, 1914.[12]

The southern textile manufacturers instantly decided to challenge the law in court. David Clark, editor of the *Southern Textile Bulletin*, led in organizing the opposition. The manufacturers decided to seek an injunction on behalf of a child who was employed in compliance with state laws but was threatened with discharge because of the federal law. They selected the federal district court in western North Carolina because they knew the judge had a predisposition to oppose federal intervention in state affairs. They believed he was reliable. Counsel then searched the mill towns for a good plaintiff and found the Dagenhart family, a father and two minor sons who were employed by the Fidelity Manufacturing Company in Charlotte. The judge, as expected, decided the law was unconstitutional. Inexplicably, given its approval of other exercises of the commerce power, on June 8, 1918, the Supreme Court by a 5–4 vote declared the act unconstitutional. The law, said Mr. Justice Day, illegally extended Congress's commerce power over production and interfered with state power to control its own manufacturing interests. The justices distinguished the case from those in which the Court had let Congress keep lottery tickets, prostitutes, and other evils out of commerce, by claiming that these things were harmful in themselves. The commodities at which this law was directed were not the evil. If any evil existed, it was child labor which resided in the states and was not in interstate commerce.[13]

The National Child Labor Committee, expecting victory, had made no plans for taking a different approach to ending child labor. Regrouping, they announced that they would either support a constitutional amendment or a new law based on the taxing power. The textile manufacturers supported the enactment of a state fourteen year minimum age requirement as a means of warding off further attack, but proposed nothing on the subject of fourteen- to sixteen-year-olds. Acknowledging the closeness of the decision and the general pattern of the Court upholding national power, the Committee decided to advance a new law to effect their goals.[14]

Several congressmen introduced constitutional amendments, but their resolutions died when the National Child Labor Committee decided to seek a new law. By September 7, 1918, the committee decided to frame a new bill based on the taxing power. A Senate bill independent of the committee, but incorporating provisions for a 10 percent tax on the net profits yearly of any concern that used child labor in violation of the Act, was added to the Revenue Bill of 1918. It passed 50–12 in the Senate on December 18, 1918. Again southern states opposed it. Southerners asserted the real intent was to overturn *Dagenhart*. When the bill passed in the House by the vote of 312–11, every one of the eleven opponents was a southern congressman.[15]

Between 1919 and 1922 while the child labor law was in effect, women gained legal protection for the right to vote and in 1918 the Children's Bureau gained a special appropriation from Congress for a "Children's Year." It engaged most women's organizations in efforts to upgrade child care, pensions for mothers, and other ameliorative measures in the states. They succeeded in increasing the number of states that had child welfare provisions from eight in 1917 to thirty-five in 1920, which formed a good basis for implementing the Sheppard-Towner Act. Also, by 1921, seventeen states had commissions drafting a children's welfare act, and in 1924 there were twenty-nine states with protective code commissions.[16]

But in order to derail the child labor protection effort, the cotton manufacturers replayed their previous tactics. They found a plaintiff, the Johnstons, father and son, in Atherton Mills in Charlotte. The mill notified Johnston that because of the new law, his son would be discharged. The same judge in the same district court was chosen to hear the case. He found the act unconstitutional but ordered only that Atherton Mills not discharge Johnston. When Johnston reached his sixteenth birthday before the case was decided, it was declared moot, and the tax went into effect. Mill owners accepted the tax as now permanent and began to make adjustments. They had decided in the interim that the tax would not really have much effect on their competitive position.[17]

But then a textile manufacturers' organization decided to find a new test vehicle to protest against having paid the tax. They believed the Supreme Court might find it illegal again. The group found a firm, the Drexel Furniture Company, in the same district court jurisdiction as in the past two cases, that agreed to become the plaintiff. The judge did the predictable: he decided the tax was illegal. Congress was trying to avoid *Dagenhart*, he said, by doing what the earlier law did but this time with a tax. The case in the Supreme Court was not helped by the fact that the solicitor general, James M. Beck, believed the tax was unconstitutional. He had expressed public approval of the *Dagenhart* decision while in private practice and deliberately took the position in *Drexel* that the Court should not simply inquire as to whether the proposal was a tax, but assess the substance of what was being taxed. In his oral argument he also seemed at times to be arguing for the mill owners instead of for the government. On May 15, 1922, three years after the tax went into effect, the Court declared it unconstitutional in an 8–1 decision. The justices concluded the tax was not an incidental restraint or a revenue measure, but a prohibitory penalty and an infringement of the powers of the state.[18]

The National Child Labor Committee had pessimistically expected the bad news this time, although hoping for the best. This time they determined to begin a constitutional amendment campaign. The decision stimulated a great deal of dissension. Many southerners noted they had opposed the Nineteenth Amendment out of fear that women in politics would stimulate child labor reform. Now they found that Florence Kelley and the majority of women reformers supported the amendment effort. But Julia Lathrop, head of the Children's Bureau, was reluctant. She thought the "popular distaste for governmental activity" would defeat their efforts in the reactionary period of the 1920s. Kelley used the League of Women Voters and the Congressional Committee to help the National Committee push the amendment along. Backed by twenty organizations, mainly women reformers, the amendment passed the Congress on June 3, 1924. Then the women formed their own organization to lobby for ratification of the child labor amendment with Mrs. Arthur Walters of the Parent-Teacher Association as chairwoman, Julia Lathrop as vice-chairwoman, Marguerite Owen, League of Women Voters, as secretary-treasurer, and other women reformers playing significant roles. However, Lathrop's pessimism was justified. Of the forty-two state legislatures that met in 1924 and 1925, only four ratified, and by 1930 the total was only six. Women were divided during the campaign. Women's reform groups were denounced as being part of an organized effort to destroy the family and promote Communism in America. The General Federation of Women's Clubs and other groups that had originally supported the amendment continued their endorsement, but weakened under the battering rhetoric of opponents to the effort. By 1925, *Survey* concluded that "Red-baiting" was a principal reason for the defeat of the amendment.[19]

The Red-baiting was spread widely by the National Association of Manufacturers, the American Medical Association, and state medical societies and affiliates. The attacks divided and confused the reform groups, which spent more time and energy repelling attacks than on trying to find ways to achieve their objectives. Conservative groups went to great lengths to link the women's efforts with bolshevism. They even accused the Women's Bureau of being pro-Communist because a bibliography for a pamphlet on maternity benefit systems of fourteen nations listed a book, for "historical interest only," on the Russian system. A book which had, in fact, been published in 1916 during the reign of Czar Nicholas II. The Red smear tactics reached their height with the publication, by the War Department, of a spider web chart purporting to be an interlocking directorate of women's organizations in America which were tied together to promote bolshevism. The supporting women's organizations were all denounced as part of the web.[20]

The child labor amendment opponents included the Sentinels of the Republic, organized in 1922 in New York City. Louis Coolidge (assistant secretary of the treasury for Theodore Roosevelt and treasurer and director of the U.S. Shoe Machine Company), its first president, named the organizaton. The Sentinels had a broad platform of preventing "useless" constitutional amendments (like the fourteenth through the nineteenth), repeal of the Sheppard-Towner Act, defeat of the child labor amendment, and the abolition of the Women's and Children's Bureaus. Their numbers included Nicholas Murray Sutter, president of Columbia University, Solicitor General James Beck, and Senators James Wadsworth and Henry Cabot Lodge. The Sentinels worked with Harriet Frothingham and Mary Kilbreth of the Women Patriots. The Patriots were comprised of the remnants of the National Organization Opposed to Woman Suffrage. Frothingham, as president of the Patriots, brought the suit against the Sheppard-Towner Act, and Solicitor General Beck encouraged Massachusetts to sue on the basis of his own belief that it was an unconstitutional invasion of states' rights. Kilbreth had been president of NAOW's, and she had denounced Harding for signing Sheppard-Towner, telling him at the time, "There are many loyal Americans, men and women, who believe that this bill, inspired by foreign experiments in Communism, and backed by the radical forces in the country, strikes at the heart of our American civilization."[21]

Because the child labor amendment passed quickly in the Congress, supporters were shocked by its resounding rejection in the states. David Clark, on behalf of southern textile manufacturers, spread editorials, propaganda, and advertisements throughout the rural press. The reformers hurt their cause by adding, in 1921, the regulation of child labor in agriculture to their objectives, expanding their original focus on the harsh conditions in industrial labor. Noting that children working in the fields, especially at planting and harvesting time, had been accepted for a long period of American history, the American Farm Bureau Federation and the Grange thereafter opposed the amendment. In the North, the Sentinels and Patriots led other conservative groups in opposition. The Sentinels insisted that the amendment would "substitute national control, directed from Washington, for local and parental control, to bring about the nationalization of the children, and to make the child the ward of the nation. It is a highly socialistic measure—an assault against individual liberty."[22]

The spider web charts and Red-baiting intimidated and dismayed the women's groups supporting the amendment. The General Federation of Women's Clubs began to waver and withdrew from the Women's Joint Congressional Committee. The National Federation of Business and Professional Women's Clubs moved from endorsement in 1924, to leaving the question to state federations in 1927.

Some women's organizations decided to stop discussing social issues and the national Women's Lawyer's Association's leadership declared that the amendment was un-American. The Daughters of the American Revolution moved from support for Sheppard-Towner and other progressive ideas, to repudiation in 1924 and a purge of moderates and liberals from the organization. They also issued a pamphlet designating ninety organizations, including the Young Women's Christian Association, the Young Men's Christian Association, the National Association for the Advancement of Colored People, and the U.S. Department of Labor as interlocked with radical groups. In addition, Jane Addams's honorary membership in the Daughters of the American Revolution was withdrawn.

When Carrie Chapman Catt tried to defend child labor amendment supporters against attacks by the DAR and other conservatives, Hermione Schwed, field secretary for the National Association for Constitutional Government, issued a pamphlet called "The Strange Case of Mrs. Carrie Chapman Catt," implying strongly that Catt was a Communist. Since Catt supported Sheppard-Towner, the child labor amendment, and other "Communist" ideas, she "intentionally or otherwise. . . has been a broadcaster for the Communists."[23]

The smear tactics and other opposition drew blood. By 1930 the social reformers were in retreat. Not only was legislation for working women out of the question, Sheppard-Towner was repealed and the child labor amendment was lost. Strong and effective mobilization by their opponents, and a generally unfavorable climate left the social reformers dismayed and in disarray. Florence Kelley asked in 1926, "Why, why did I ever help to start the National Child Labor Committee?"[24]

Supporters lost the amendment as antireform sentiment prevailed, unlike the period of progressive reform in the early years of the National Child Labor Committee. But the child labor reformers ultimately achieved their objective, because during the emergency of the Depression, the Fair Labor Standards Act included provisions they had sought earlier regulating child labor. They had made the case for ending the abuses as a societal concern, but their goal was obtained without amending the Constitution. Their repeated efforts to gain legislation reminded some people that legislation could remedy the problem. A newly constituted Supreme Court overruled *Hammer* v. *Dagenhart* and upheld the new law.[25]

For supporters of other controversial amendments, including ERA, their experience demonstrates the importance of timing as well as the necessity for developing a state consensus first on major substantive issues if an amendment is to be achieved. If proponents had really believed that only a constitutional amendment could solve the problem, they should have kept to an amendment strategy before proposing legislative solutions. They also should have focused single-mindedly on the struggle for an amendment when their movement was at full tide. The Russian Revolution and the anti-Communist smears created an environment which would not have existed with such intensity fifteen years earlier. But most important, they underestimated the ferocity of their opponents' campaign and were unprepared for the Red smears and charges of anti-Americanism. They undervalued how effective such propaganda could be in denying consensus in the states and were too optimistic because of their rapid success in the Congress. They needed a carefully planned state ratification strategy, expecting the worst before congressional enactment. Quick passage in the Congress would have been good only if state consensus already existed, not when it needed to be developed. However, their strategy was compromised from the beginning because they were never quite sure they needed to amend the Constitution. They underestimated their opponents, implemented a state ratification strategy too late and after too much negative information had been disseminated. Later controversial amendment proponents would need to learn the lessons demonstrated by successful earlier substantive amendment supporters while avoiding the mistakes of the child labor advocates.

ERA: Approval and Early Ratification Campaigns 6

As they pursued the quest for the ERA, the proponents seemed to be unaware of everything that could have been learned from history about how to achieve ratification of a controversial Constitutional amendment. The factors of time, demonstrating necessity, regional and state diversity as elements in gaining consensus in the states, the positive influence of negative Supreme Court decisions, the expectation of disinformation spread by the opponents—all proved crucial in one or another of the earlier campaigns, and they all proved to be crucial in the defeat of the Equal Rights Amendment that was introduced in 1972. Most especially they seemed not to learn from the failure of the child labor amendment.

Immediately following the ratification of the Nineteenth Amendment, congressmen, worried about how women would vote, passed a number of bills, supported by women in the 1920s, in addition to the Sheppard-Towner Act of 1921. These included the Packers and Stockyards Bill of 1921, to increase consumer protection; the Cable Act of 1922, to protect citizenship rights of American women who married foreigners; and the Lehlback Act of 1924, upgrading the merit system in the civil service. Unlike other social reform issues, the National Woman's party was interested in the Cable Act, in part because important members, including Consuelo Vanderbilt and Harriet Blatch, had previously lost their citizenship through marriage to aliens. But it soon became clear that women did not vote as a bloc and did not base their votes entirely upon women's issues. Consequently, by the 1930s, women reformers experienced two major failures in the programs they supported: the child labor amendment and Sheppard-Towner extension in 1929. Divided by attacks of their opponents, accused of anti-Americanism, torn apart over how to protect working women from long hours and poor wages while working for equal treatment, the women's movement staggered along from 1929 to the 1940s.[1]

When the National Woman's party proposed to move aggressively for an Equal Rights Amendment in 1923, the goal became immediately controversial. After achieving suffrage, party lobbyists worked in state legislatures to eliminate specific sex discrimination but achieved little success. A federal constitutional amendment seemed a logical next step to Alice Paul and her party, but not to those who wanted the vote but did not want women and men to be treated equally in other cases. To those reformers who saw suffrage as a means of obtaining social reforms which in limited ways would treat women differently, the amendment was regarded as particularly pernicious. Although many of the women on both sides had shared in the suffrage fight, and efforts were made to heal their differences, they were unsuccessful. When the supporters of suffrage shifted ground, emphasizing the lack of change that would occur, to gain approval of the Nineteenth Amendment, they gave credence to the view that they accepted no change in women's traditional role and place in society and their differentiation from men. When Alice Paul and the Woman's party proceeded with the ERA and attacked special legislation for women, they were criticized by reformers such as Catt, Florence Kelly, and Jane Addams who had supported woman suffrage. The reformers had another agenda. When the New Deal was introduced, female and male social workers and reformers who gathered in Washington to help address the Depression found a warm welcome from Eleanor Roosevelt. New Deal programs were defined as helping the family. Women were appointed to policy-making posts in larger numbers, including Frances Perkins as secretary of labor, the first female cabinet member (for whom the Department of Labor's main building is named today).[2]

Whatever success women found in helping to implement the New Deal, economic equality, in terms of the employment of women in jobs outside the home, did not come easily between 1920 and 1940. Large numbers of women, even those who were married and middle-income, continued to work in factories and, increasingly, in clerical occupations. They believed their families needed the increased status their incomes could provide. Between 1930 and 1940, despite the Depression, the number of married women in the labor force increased by about 50 percent. Career women found great difficulty in trying to break down traditional barriers against entry into certain fields. In industry, reformers campaigned increasingly in the decades after 1890 for protective hours and wages legislation for working women. After the *Muller* case in 1908, the effort proceeded apace. But a 1923 decision, *Adkins* v. *Children's Hospital*, in which the Supreme Court struck down the District of Columbia's minimum wage law for women, was a telling blow. The National Woman's party filed a brief asking that the minimum wage be outlawed as inconsistent with the

idea of women's equality under the law, engendering outrage from
the social reformers. The Court's majority opinion seemed to agree
more with the Woman's party than the reformers. The justices ad-
verted to the presence of the Nineteenth Amendment as sufficient
protection for women to vote equality for themselves without the need
for special legislative efforts. The New Deal Court changed the situation by overruling *Adkins* and upholding federal and state minimum
wage laws for men and women which gave new impetus to such legislation. As a result of protective legislation and the legalization of
union contracts, and the active efforts to recruit women by the Congress of Industrial Organizations, the plight of women in industry
was improved. Still, by 1939, twenty-one states had no minimum wage
laws for women, thirty had no eight hour day statutes, and the Congress of Industrial Organizations' activities bore fruit only later.[3]

In the professions, between 1920 and 1940, female employment
and female college education increased substantially. But women still
were denied top positions and had unequal earnings and status as
compared with men. Younger women seemed to be content with the
pace of progress. Indeed, an increase in sexual freedom proceeded
with a reaffirmation of traditional male and female roles. Women
would principally be wives and mothers, and a career must not interfere with those assumptions. Even the curriculum of women's colleges changed to emphasize the value of domesticity. Women's
magazines also praised the virtues of homemaking as the primary role
for women while they attacked female involvement in areas outside
of women's sphere. During the Depression, even Secretary of Labor
Frances Perkins denounced married women workers for taking jobs
from men who needed them.[4]

The National Woman's party achieved some success with ERA despite the opposition of women reformers, the controversy over the
party's opposition to protective legislation, and a general lack of support for the issue. In 1936 a House subcommittee endorsed the ERA
amendment. In 1938 the Senate Judiciary Committee reported it out
to the floor, and the Republican party supported it in the election of
1940. But the opposition to it was so great that these small successes
were all the NWP had to show for its efforts. An additional burden
was that the Woman's party position came to be identified with the
Republican party, which offended Democratic partisans, including
Eleanor Roosevelt.[5]

World War II drastically changed the situation of women. The demand for workers increased the numbers of women in the labor force
by over 50 percent. Unionization of women, leading to increased
wages, and the number of wives working increased enormously.
Women also saw increased employment in business and benefited

from upward mobility. Black women, already more often workers, were able to move from domestic service and fieldwork into manufacturing jobs, which paid higher wages. But equal pay and assignment to top jobs remained elusive for them.[6]

Child care for the children of working mothers became a major issue for women as stories of latch key children proliferated. Some cities developed extensive after-school programs and opened child care centers for pre-school children. Infant schools and nurseries had existed since at least the 1830s. In 1896, a National Federation of Day Nurseries was organized to improve standards of care. The day nursery was first included in the National Conference of Social Work in 1919. By the 1930s, women workers emphasized the contributions of day care centers to family life. During the Depression, federally financed nursery schools were established under the Works Progress Administration. The purpose was to provide work for the professional and non-professional employees, but the by-product was care for children. In 1942 the federal government decided these schools were no longer needed as a source of employment and proposed reducing services to provide only for children of women working in war industries. Governmental response to the increased needs for services during the war was dictated not only by financial considerations, but also by a view that women's primary duty was to care for children. For example, the Children's Bureau and Women's Bureau opposed child care centers as an incentive for women to leave the home. In 1943, the Roosevelt administration reluctantly ruled that Lanham Act funds for construction of wartime facilities could be used for day care operations for war workers. But the application and approval of procedures for implementation was so arduous that it was difficult to use the funds for this purpose. A Women's Bureau survey noted that no adequate provisions for day care were ever made during the war.[7]

When the war ended, after a period of dislocation many women, even married women and those over thirty-five, continued to work outside their homes. But discrimination in wages and in the professions continued. Also, the nebulous child care efforts were officially ended by the federal government in 1946. Most of the nurseries in the states closed operations, but in California where women were still regarded as needed in the electronics and aircraft industries, the Lanham Act funds were continued on a "temporary" basis. In New York City, not designated a war impact area, no Lanham Act funds were received. When the WPA funds were withdrawn, parents, professionals, and labor unions successfully petitioned Mayor Fiorello LaGuardia to keep city-supported nurseries open. Many people expressed the opinion that the Aid to Families with Dependent Children program enacted under the Social Security Act of 1935 was better for women and children because the mothers could then stay at home while receiving benefits. One great change was more public acknowledgment that women who worked often did so out of necessity instead of desire. In 1900 most women who worked had been single, young, poor and/or black. By 1950, while blacks were still disproportionately represented, most woman workers were married and middle-aged, and substantial numbers came from the middle class.[8]

But the war did not help the advocates of the Equal Rights Amendment. Both parties supported it, as did President Harry Truman. But prominent women, like Eleanor Roosevelt, still opposed it as inimical to protective legislation. In August 1946, the Senate approved the amendment by 38–35, far short of the two-thirds majority needed for adoption. In 1950, Senator Carl Hayden of Arizona added a rider that no protective legislation would be affected and the Equal Rights Amendment passed 63–19. It passed again with his amendment in 1953. Hayden deliberately added the riders in order to divide the amendment's supporters, and these tactics delayed serious consideration of the unamended version of the Equal Rights Amendment.[9]

The late 1940s and the 1950s saw increasing public discussion of women's appropriate place in view of the fact that so many women worked outside the home. Expressions of bewilderment existed, most often among middle-class white women. Black women, who more often had always had to work, had long been accustomed to balancing the imperatives of family life with work outside the home and did not seem confused about the transformations. Many of them longed not to work and worried about the lack of opportunity for black men, who were often in no position to support a family. Poor white women, even when they had to work, regarded it as antithetical to their preferred role of not working when they had husbands who could support them.[10]

The 1960s brought a revival of the women's rights movement and more insistence on changed social and legal rights and responsibilities. The fact of women's involvement in the civil rights movement and the anti-war movement and their changed role in the economy created a social context in which many women became active supporters of enhanced legislation for themselves. The agenda they pursued had already been well established in the long history of women's rights activism.[11]

In *The Feminine Mystique* (1963) when Betty Friedan summed up female discontent with being regarded as only a wife or mother, she found an immediate positive response. She and others who wrote about the issue described the main problem as the denial of a woman's opportunity to fulfill her own identity and needs, whatever they were. They complained that for too long biology, for women, had been regarded as destiny. Careers, which large numbers of women already had, were fine and could expand a woman's horizons, but they were adjuncts to family responsibilities and not to be taken seriously. The women's movement developed throughout the 1960s and until the enactment of ERA in 1972 with little attention paid to challenges to their complaints or to the fact that many women did not agree with the view that their roles should change, even when they had already changed substantially. Many women asserted that they did not want to work outside the home even when they had to, and many who were housewives only did not have to work or had neither the skills nor the training to pursue professional careers. On the other hand, many women, especially in minority groups, who had always had to work while experiencing underemployment, exploitation, and neglect of family did not see being permitted to work as a major objective. *The Feminine Mystique* was not some new phenomenon. Advocates were repeating and extending the historical arguments for a change in women's place, which in turn generated the same historical counter-arguments that had been made traditionally against the women's rights movement: that it threatened home and family.[12]

When the Civil Rights Act of 1964, Title VII, to end race discrimination in employment came before the Congress, the results gave impetus to the developing women's rights movement. Women reformers played key roles in amending the legislation to cover sex discrimination. Congressman Howard W. Smith was chairman of the Rules Committee. Some thought he introduced the provisions of sex equality in order to kill the bill, but Congresswoman Martha Griffiths (D, Mich.) is generally considered its author. When he introduced the bill, Smith said he wanted to address "the imbalance of spinsters." Martha Griffiths defeated the AFL-CIO and others who felt the addition of sex would kill the bill. Griffiths said when she learned "that a woman newspaper reporter had asked Howard Smith of Virginia to offer such an amendment and he had agreed," she decided to let him offer it. She thought Smith had miscalculated. Some conservatives would vote for it because he had offered it, and she could persuade others to join in its passage. As she put it, "I used Smith."[13]

After the bill was passed, women were concerned that in focusing on the rights of blacks, the Equal Employment Opportunity Commission would ignore complaints from non-black women unless they had a strong advocacy group such as the NAACP and the NAACP Legal Defense and Educational Fund that advocated black equality. In 1966, at a meeting of the Third National Conference on the Commission on the Status of Women, concern about enforcement of sex discrimination provisions in Title VII of the Civil Rights Act of 1964 led a group, which included Betty Friedan, to found the National

Organization for Women (NOW). NOW focused, as the National Association had during the suffrage fight, on change within the system. Legislation would create equality. Women's liberation groups, growing out of the peace, civil rights, and student movements, focused on consciousness raising, female-male differences, and in some cases, the need to change the entire economic and social structure of the society. All groups agreed on some issues, including an end to job discrimination in pay and work opportunities; an end to assumptions that women should do all of the housework, or be principally responsible for raising children; and the repeal of abortion laws to provide freedom for women to choose whether or not to bear a child.[14]

The women's movement had far-reaching immediate results. Some women who did not need to work for economic reasons took jobs for reasons of personal development; women who already worked sought enriched opportunities. Religious women fought for roles from which they had been traditionally excluded in the churches, including becoming ministers. Many women who said in the polls that they wanted to marry, began saying that they also needed to work.[15]

The efforts of those who had supported ERA for years before the contemporary women's movement began, started to bear fruit in this more receptive climate. By the late 1960s, ERA was brought to the floor of the House and enthusiastically supported, although not passed. Federal civil rights laws began to emphasize anti-discrimination against women. Abortion reform laws were passed in several states, politicians started appointing more women to administrative posts and in their campaigns and campaigned on platforms including women's rights planks, as they had in the immediate aftermath of the 19th amendment. Employment opportunity received great public support as issues such as abortion and child care remained particularly controversial. To opponents, these goals seemed to threaten the very foundations of society by changing assumptions about women's relationships with children and families.[16]

In the 1960's some women's rights advocates continued to believe that complete equality for women could be gradually gained through the 14th amendment. The President's Commission on the Status of Women (1963) concluded that an equal rights amendment was not needed because equality could come through the 14th and 15th amendments. Hopes that the Supreme Court would move in this direction were improved when in 1971 the Court invaded states' rights by invalidating an Idaho law giving preference to men over women as administrators of estates. However, those who feared that such a process would never occur, and if it did would be long in coming, noted that the Court refused to use "strict scrutiny" as a standard in assessing the legality of sex discrimination, as it did with race legislation under the 14th amendment. But as polls began showing an overwhelming national consensus about the need for women's equality, many feminists believed that it would be easy to get ERA enacted. By 1970, Presidents Johnson and Nixon endorsed it as did the President's Task Force on the Status of Women and the Citizens' Advisory Council on the Status of Women. Some of the unions and the Women's Bureau which had held back in defense of protective legislation also came to support it.[17]

The legislative history of the ERA enacted in 1972 began in May 1970 when the Senate Subcommittee on Constitutional Amendments held the first hearing since 1955 on the subject. Forty-two witnesses (including lawyers, legislators, and women's groups), most of whom supported the amendment, testified. In the House, Congresswoman Martha Griffiths of Michigan succeeded in forcing the amendment out of the House Judiciary Committee on a discharge petition. The chairman of the Judiciary Committee, Congressman Emmanuel D. Celler of New York, had long been opposed to the amendment. After an hour of floor debate on August 10, 1970, it passed 350–15. The Senate took up the bill on the floor and debated it for several days in October 1970. Much of the discussion concerned whether ERA would require women to be drafted. On October 13, 1970, the Senate adopted a bill exempting women from the draft by a vote of 36–33. Although over eighty senators, more than the two-thirds required for passage, were listed as sponsors (some of whom probably signed on to get political credit from women supporters of the amendment), no action was taken on ERA in the Ninety-first Congress. In the Ninety-second Congress, hearings were held on the reintroduced bill in the House Judiciary Committee in March 1971. The Committee voted it out with the confining amendment that it would "not impair the validity of any law of the United States which exempts a person from compulsory military service or any other law of the United States or any State which reasonably promotes the health and safety of the people." The committee amendment was rejected 104–254, and ERA was passed 354–23.[18]

In the Senate, the Subcommittee on Constitutional Amendments reported to the committee an ERA with an amendment that "neither the United States nor any State shall make any legal distinctions between the rights and responsibilities of male and female persons unless such distinction is based on physiological or functional differences between them." The full committee rejected this language 15–1 and also rejected sections proposed to modify equality in matters of child support, protective labor legislation, sex crimes, privacy, the admissions policies of higher education institutions, the draft, and military service. The Senate approved the unamended version of ERA by a

vote of 84–8 on March 22, 1972. The greatest number of votes the
restrictive floor amendments received was eighteen. The consensus
necessary to gain congressional passage had been developed carefully
as reflected in polls, organized women's activities, and the attention
of the politicians. In the euphoria over the overwhelming passage in
the Congress, the amendment's supporters predicted quick ratification. But in their jubilation, they failed to note carefully the arguments
made by opponents, or to develop in advance a strategy to counteract
them should they later gain support. They also failed to note that
several separate consensuses would be needed in at least thirty-eight
states, and opponents had the easier task—they only needed to keep
thirteen states from ratifying. They did not need a national consensus.
ERA proponents also did not reflect on the role women and family
issues played in the fight over suffrage, Prohibition, and the child
labor amendments, and the difficulties those amendments could not
overcome in much of the South. But in the glow of congressional
passage, amassing thirty-eight state ratifications seemed easy.[19]

An article published in the *Yale Law Journal* in 1971 to provide a
comprehensive supportive theory for ERA was distributed by Congresswoman Martha Griffiths and inserted in the Congressional Record by Senator Birch Bayh, Chair of the Senate Subcommittee on
Constitutional Amendments. One of the most persuasive witnesses
during both the House and Senate hearings was one of the article's
authors, Yale Professor Thomas Emerson. The importance of the
article went without saying, but certain statements (for example, that
"The major political action—passage and ratification of the amendment—can be accomplished by a strong nationwide campaign of limited duration," and "the amending process is designed to elicit national
ratification for changes in basic governing values,") did little to clarify
what was really needed. Not a nationwide campaign, but several dis-
crete campaigns directed regionally or state by state were needed for
success in the effort. National support was not the only goal, but
adoption by separate state ratifications, each of which would require
a different kind of consensus concerning the amendment's necessity.[20]

The ratification deadline of March 22, 1979, set by the Congress
in 1972 for ERA made ratification problematical, although it appeared
simple to proponents. Article V made no provision as to time limits
for ratification. In *Dillon* v. *Gloss* in 1921, the Supreme Court had
decided Congress could prescribe a reasonable time if it chose to do
so. In the case of the Eighteenth Amendment, the first amendment
to have a prescribed ratification time included, the Court found seven
years to be a reasonable time. The recent example of the unratified
child labor amendment may have led Congress to put a time limit on
ratification of the Eighteenth Amendment and thereafter on the twen-

tieth, twenty-first, and twenty-second. Since that time, as before the eighteenth, no time limit had been placed on ratification—until ERA. Given the political, public, and legal support for their amendment, ERA supporters believed the approval of thirty-eight states would come easily. Indeed, twenty-two state legislatures approved it in 1972. But then the slow, trench warfare began, and by November 1978, only thirteen additional states had ratified and four had rescinded their approvals.[21]

In Alaska and Hawaii, which ratified quickly, the wounds of the earlier Prohibition, suffrage, and child labor debates had never been inflicted. These two were not even admitted to statehood until the 1950s. Most of the other states that ratified without much conflict in 1972 and 1973 had already resolved their positions in favor of women's rights by enacting equal protective labor legislation for men and women. The states that did not ratify in 1972 and 1973 were the same ones that had not enacted such protective labor legislation, except for Illinois, in which peculiar local circumstances (including the need for a three-fifths vote in the legislature to ratify) should have led proponents to worry about approval.[22]

The supporters of ERA, sure of success, did not make any major allocation of resources to ratification in the first year. The only organized resistance in the congressional debates seemed to come from established, politically conservative groups and Happiness of Womanhood (HOW). But by the end of the first spate of ratifications, numerous groups organized to repeat the negative arguments about military service, forcing housewives to work and contribute one half of family support, and reducing women's rights under state domestic codes and labor laws that had been raised in the congressional hearings. These groups focused particularly on the unratified states but also made efforts to gain rescissions in the ratified ones.[23]

The opposition gained strength rapidly. In 1972 the platform of the American party, which had nominated George Wallace for president in 1968, denounced ERA as a "socialistic plan to destroy the home." The John Birch Society thundered that it was part of "communist plans . . . to reduce human beings to the level of animals." HOW president and founder, Jacquie Davison, wife of a San Diego chiropractor, insisted ERA would legitimate homosexuality and permit homosexuals to marry and even to adopt children.[24]

Direct action on both sides quickly became the rule along with traditional lobbying tactics. In Louisiana, a group of anti-ERA women broke windows and spray painted "PIG" on the New Orleans homes of two legislative opponents, leaving behind threatening letters made from newspaper clippings. In Virginia, two ERA supporters were arrested for disorderly conduct, trespassing, and assaulting a police officer after the amendment was defeated in a House committee. In 1972 in California, state Senator James Mills, who had stalled ERA in the Senate Rules Committee, was subjected to demonstrations and interruptions at his public appearances. ERA passed out of his committee and was quickly ratified. Thereafter parades, rallies, and pickets accompanied the pro and anti drives in the states.[25]

In some states where quick ratification took place, there was little lobbying at the time or discussion of the issues. In Texas, the eighth state to ratify in March 1972, the legislators did not engage in much discussion at all. The ratification took place just before a primary, and legislators thought it was less risky to go ahead and pass it than to wait for public reaction.[26]

By 1973, several effective anti-ERA ad hoc groups emerged, the most prominent of which was Phyllis Schlafly's Stop ERA. Republican conservative, former vice-president of the National Federation of Republican Women, founder of the Eagles are Flying, author or co-author of several books (including Barry Goldwater's *A Choice, Not an Echo*), and editor and publisher of *Phyllis Schlafly's Report*, she proved to be the most visible and effective leader of the anti-ERA forces. In February 1972, her entire *Report* was devoted to "What's Wrong with 'Equal Rights' for Women," as her first public statement on ERA. In late 1972 she started Stop ERA using the slogan, "You can't fool Mother Nature," and by February 1973 had several thousand active members in twenty-six states, mostly in the South and Midwest. Schlafly focused her fire on Section II of the proposed ERA, as taking away power from the state legislatures that were being asked to ratify and granting possible federal control over traditional family matters. She seemed to know better than the ERA proponents where to focus her efforts and that she needed only thirteen non-ratifying states to win. Unlike the national groups that supported ERA, which already had chapters they would use in the states, the anti groups organized from the grassroots, building chapters. They issued much less literature and were vague about their financial support base.[27]

After the fact of congressional enactment, the national ERA organizations slowly mobilized for the state efforts. An ERA ratification council of about thirty proponent groups, formed shortly after passage, consisted mainly of congressional lobbyists and did very little. Not until April 1973 did the council appoint an "ERA Action Committee" (composed of delegates from the National Woman's party, Common Cause, the League of Women Voters, and Business and Professional Women's Clubs) to formulate a national ratification strategy. By June, the Committee had developed assignments for constituent organizations. For example, NWPC would try to gain the election of proponents in the legislatures. NOW would bring pressure on legislative opponents and use direct action in raising ERA in election campaigns. Common Cause would produce and distribute issue papers and arguments, and the LWV would train lobbyists. But not much coordination occurred. Thereafter, "Operation Task Force" was organized, including many of the same groups. From 1973 to 1974 they spent about $200,000 on salaries, staff, travel, and mailings to help in ratification.[28]

By 1974 the groups understood well the real difficulties they faced and how little time they had left. The National Federation of Business and Professional Women hired a prominent Republican consulting firm, Bailey, Deardorff, and Eyre to do a case study of the seventeen unratified states. Their report advised focusing on ten states where chances in 1975 seemed good. A fund, and a new coordinating organization, ERA America, was opened in January 1976 and co-chaired by Democrat Liz Carpenter and Republican Elly Peterson. This coordinating group, funded by proponent groups and the separate groups, continued the push for ERA.

By mid-1974 statewide pro-ERA groups, many of which had staff and active volunteer supporters, existed in fourteen of the seventeen unratified states. In the already ratified states not much organization occurred until rescission efforts, which succeeded in Nebraska in 1973, in Idaho in 1972, in Tennessee in 1974, and in Kentucky in 1978, were well underway.[29]

In Illinois, a hotly contested unratified state, several ERA coalitions developed after its 1972 failure in the legislature. After the amendment's defeat again in 1974, the League of Women Voters and NOW led in setting up a state ratification council to focus on areas outside Chicago. In 1976 all groups supporting the amendment organized ERA-Illinois with a full-time director and staff. A major problem was the AFL-CIO, which did practically nothing to help gain ratification. In the Illinois House of Representatives, ERA became an issue in a fight between black legislators from Chicago and the city's Democratic leadership, over their power to represent the city's interests in the House. The black legislators, dismayed because the city's Democratic politicians provided support for ERA in exchange for a deal on their candidates for leadership in the House, voted against the amendment. Because the women's movement had ignored the necessity for developing grassroots support in the black community, the legislators did not fear criticism in their districts.[30]

The anti-ERA groups in Illinois consisted not just of Schlafly and Stop ERA, but also NCCW, the John Birch Society, HOW, and a group called Right To Be a Woman. They insisted they funded themselves and operated independently. Opponents derived high social status from husbands in professions and business, but a few were profes-

sional women. The proponents were almost all employed, and most
held business or professional jobs. Many of the antis had already been
active in community causes, as had the proponents. In the legislature,
the fact that national leaders supported ERA was used by opponents
to argue that the legislature should not allow itself to be controlled
by outsiders. The opponents were helped by divisions in the Democratic party, by their alliance with conservative Republicans, and by
the failure of organized labor to help the proponents. In fact, the
downstate rural vote which had also voted against child labor law and
for Prohibition, was still there in residue form, although a poll of all
the counties in 1974 showed 60 percent of the public polled, for
ERA.[33]

State by state the failure to gain ratification, although including
peculiar local circumstances (such as the Illinois requirement that
three-fifths of each House is necessary instead of a simple majority),
proceeded from the same problems. There was a basic liberal-con-
servative political split, a regional split, a divergence of attitudes toward women, and differences of ideology. The proponents needed
much more in the way of resources and organization because they
had to be active in so many states, but they did too little, too late. They
were in the defensive position of trying to subvert the opponents, led
by Schlafly, because they did not pay careful attention to the necessity
for a state-by-state consensus. They then had to play catch-up. They
did not understand that the issues of the role of women, abortion,
the draft, and the family would find so much opposition that they
had to be debated and combatted affirmatively.

As the ERA proponents gathered at the federally financed 1977
International Women's Year Conference in Houston and endorsed
homosexual rights and other controversial resolutions on national
television, they helped to make the case for ERA opponents. Instead
of giving ammunition to the opponents, they needed to de-emphasize
the divisive issues. They also needed more time to lay the groundwork,
by persuading state legislators or electing replacements for the re-
calcitrant ones, and for giving junior legislators time to gain seniority.
The quick strike successes of the first year were really unhelpful, for
they generated much unjustified optimism. The proponents were
lulled into a false sense of security while the opposition gained time
to organize. In general, ERA proponents were completely disorgan-
ized for a successful state ratification effort. When, in an effort to
demonstrate political clout, NOW called for an economic boycott of
unratified states in 1977, it was already too late. By August 1978, 202
organizations had voted to hold conventions only in states that had
ratified. Chicago, Kansas City, Las Vegas, Miami, Atlanta, and New
Orleans lost, altogether, in excess of $100 million in convention busi-

ness over the next several years. The support for ERA in these states was mainly in the cities already, so the boycott did little to get rural interests to agree to ratify.[32]

When there is no conflict over an issue and some perceived advantages to supporting it, legislators—whatever their personal views—will often vote for it, as they did in the early ratifying states. But when conflict arises, they often try to avoid conflict by doing nothing. In this case classic legislative behavior meant not ratifying and, if they really were philosophically opposed to begin with, voting in the negative. Ideology, interparty rivalry, and partisan politics, then, may all come into play. Then only if minds can be changed, as legislators perceive they will lose office by opposition, will they vote positively. Given the deep divisions among women in the nonratifying states, legislators did not need to fear retribution for voting against ERA, and not many minds were changed.[33]

ERA: Extension, Rescission, and Failure

7

ERA proponents faced an increasingly uphill battle despite the fact that thirty-five states had ratified by 1978. Time was running out, and some states that had already ratified were rescinding their ratifications. The longer the debate continued, the weaker the chance for approval seemed. Proponents had to fight on three fronts. They needed to gain an extension of time for ratification in the Congress, which would reflect how much national consensus still existed. They had to prevent further rescissions, which meant keeping the consensus they had achieved in some states. And they needed to develop a consensus in three more states to gain ratification. They succeeded in gaining an extension and avoided a definitive decision about rescission, but failed in their overall objective of obtaining ratification of ERA. In fact, the debate over the legality of extensions and rescissions helped to erode consensus because if there had been sufficient support for ERA, the issue of rescissions and extension would never have arisen.

In 1978, when the proponents of ERA knew they could not achieve thirty-eight state ratifications by 1979, they succeeded, on August 15, in gaining an extension of time in the House by a vote of 233–189 and by a vote in the Senate of 60–36, but not without difficulty.[1] During the congressional debate and until June 30, 1982, when the extension expired, scholars continued to argue the constitutionality of the extension. In addition, they argued over whether the rescissions were valid when made and whether they would remain valid during the extension period. The arguments remain of interest because they shed light on the difficulties involved in gaining and keeping consensus for the passage of ERA. No prior amendment's time limit for passage had ever been extended, but extensions had been attempted. Opponents of the ERA extension argued that state legislatures which ratified ERA manifested no intention to have their ratifications remain in force, either automatically or at the option of Congress, beyond March 22, 1979. These opponents insisted that the validity of the amendment was conditional on the time limit of seven years. They saw nothing in the text or history of Article V to give Congress the power to change any part of the language agreed to by a state, and seven years was part of the ERA language. In addition, some scholars pointed out that legally an offer and acceptance of agreed-upon terms is required before any contract is valid. ERA ratification, according to this view, was a contract. Therefore, states could not be regarded as contracting for something not in the agreed upon terms. The agreed upon terms included a seven year limit. When seven years passed, all pre-existing ratifications expired.[2]

The proponents of extension, on the other hand, insisted that Congress had plenary power over the ratification process based on the text and history of Article V. The time limit was not a condition of the contract but only a guideline which Congress could change. They accepted the contract model, but the contract was only for the substance of the amendment—equality of rights.[3] Furthermore, states cannot ratify conditionally because that would be no ratification at all. Once ratified nothing else is necessary. The opponents of extension did not prevail, in part because Congress, in enacting the extension, acknowledged the effect of *Coleman* v. *Miller*, decided by the Supreme Court in 1939. The Court held that most questions dealing with the amending process, including the validity of state ratifications, must be decided by the Congress alone.[4]

In addition to the issue of extensions, the question of rescissions remains important because it is likely to arise again if ERA is passed by the Congress, and the ratification process begins. It may then, again become a matter of great controversy. James Madison, who was largely responsible for the content of Article V, wrote in regard to ratification of the Constitution itself that, "The Constitution requires an adoption in toto and for ever." But he also wrote that "[c]ompacts must be reciprocal."[5]

Proponents of rescission argued that Madison's statements meant that if a state legislature ratified thinking it could rescind, then rescission became part of the original ratification compact. However, opponents pointed out that this position begs the question. Later rescission in no way indicates that legislators believed that when they ratified they could rescind. Also, if a legislature ratified under conditions, including existing Court precedents, which required that their ratification would be final, either the ratification is valid because a mistake of law is no excuse, or their original ratification would have been invalid because they conditioned it in a way that was impermissibly legally. But no evidence was proferred that any legislators believed their ratifications were invalid when voted. From their standpoint, the ratifications had to be regarded as valid.[6]

The issues of ratification and rescission had arisen before the ERA controversy, in connection with the Thirteenth, Fourteenth, and Fifteenth Amendments, and a number of precedents were established. The governor of Kentucky, when commenting on his state legislature's rejection of the Thirteenth Amendment, stated in 1865, "[n]othing but ratification forecloses the right of action. When ratified all power is expended. Until ratified the right to ratify remains," a confirmation of the Madisonian view. With the Fourteenth Amendment, twenty-nine states ratified by July 1868, but two, Ohio and New Jersey, had passed rescinding legislation. Congress passed a resolution declaring the amendment validly adopted including Ohio and New Jersey. Commentators have argued that the ratification was invalid because the rescissions were ignored and because ratification was a condition for readmission to the Union for the seceded southern states. But the Supreme Court indicated in *White* v. *Hart* in 1871 that the coercion argument was invalid because congressional action "upon the subject cannot be inquired into,"[7]

The objecting states on the Thirteenth, Fourteenth, and Fifteenth Amendments could have refused to ratify and awaited admission by some other method, but they did not. New York rescinded its ratification of the Fifteenth Amendment, but was included in the list of ratifying states certified by the secretary of state. But the New York vote was not needed to obtain three-fourths consensus for ratification. Also a report of the Senate reviewed the subject and concluded in 1973 that "Congress previously has taken the position that having once ratified an amendment, a State may not rescind." The Senate passed a bill permitting rescissions twice, in 1971 and 1973, but the House had, by 1978, refused to do so.[8]

In connection with the Eighteenth and Nineteenth Amendments, rescission issues were raised indirectly, and the results were consistent with the Madisonian view that they were impermissible. If rescissions had been attempted during the extension period for ERA, they would be just as invalid as attempted rescissions during the original seven year period because of the plenary power of the Congress over the amending process. The question was aired fully during the hearings over the ERA extension and the legislative history supports the view that Congress continues to regard rescission as null and void.[9]

Jules Gerard's study of thirty-two ratifying states found that twenty included the time limit in their discussions, four made no reference to it in their ratification documents, four mentioned it without saying why, and four mentioned it as an inducement for ratifying. Gerard concluded that at least twenty-eight states had relied on the time limit and, therefore, ought to be considered unratified if the extension went into effect. But critics of this conclusion pointed out that the state legislatures involved did not insist that they would not have ratified without the limit. If they had insisted, then ratification would have been invalid in the first place for attempting to attach conditions, consistent with the Madisonian view that conditional ratifications are not ratifications at all.[10]

Those who continued to argue that rescissions were valid and congressional extensions invalid could take comfort from a 1981 district court opinion by Judge Callister in *Idaho* v. *Freeman*. Judge Callister discounted the history of earlier rescissions by concluding that Congress has never decisively resolved the issue, therefore, no precedent was established. He used a 1974 three-judge appellate court decision in which Judge Stevens (now Supreme Court Justice Stevens) wrote that cases since *Coleman* v. *Miller* (1939) had enlarged the number and kind of issues the courts could decide without worrying that they involved political questions. Therefore, the courts, he asserted, can decide Article V questions. Judge Callister concluded that the statements in *Coleman* that the courts should not decide rescission and ratification decisions were "dicta" and not part of the official holding in the case. Therefore, courts did not have to follow this doctrine.[11]

Callister asserted that only the states can determine whether there is sufficient "local consensus" for an amendment. If they review the question and vote to rescind their decisions, there is no longer a valid consensus if three-fourths have not ratified in the interim.

> If Congress could refuse to recognize a state's rescission, it would mean that Congress would supplant the expression of the people's representative with its own assessment of consent by holding that the prior expression of consent is valid.

On extension, he stated that

> . . . if the Congress chooses to fix a time period by making it part of its proposal to the states, that determination of a time period becomes an integral part of the proposed mode of ratification. Once the proposal has been formulated and sent to the states, the time period cannot be changed any more than the entity designated to ratify could be changed from the state legislatures to a state convention or vice versa.

Callister's decision was appealed, but before the Supreme Court could decide the appeal, the time of the extension had passed without ERA ratification. Therefore, the Supreme Court acknowledged on October 4, 1982, that the case was moot.[12]

Because the Congress has reiterated its understanding that extensions are permissible and rescissions impermissible, *Idaho* v. *Freeman* remains only an unimplemented district court decision contrary to existing Supreme Court precedent, and there is less reason now than ever for a state to attempt rescission of a ratification of an amendment. Instead of relying on rescissions, proponents and opponents of any amendment would be well advised to make their case during the ratification discussions and then abandon them if a ratification is enacted by the state legislatures. The debate over rescissions and extensions seemed only to complicate the problems of determining whether new ratifications could be achieved before the June 30, 1982, deadline. The complications did not help the proponents. Thirty-five states had ratified by the 1979 deadline, but not another was gained in the next three years.[13]

The tide had turned definitively, and seeking an extension only made matters worse. Despite the boycotting of Chicago by conventioneers, a Mother's Day march in Chicago of nearly 100,000 for ERA, and lobbying by saleswomen, teachers, housewives, nurses, executives, union members, NOW leaders, letters, and mailgrams the Illinois legislature, in June 1980, refused for the seventh time to ratify ERA.[14]

The year 1980 saw a series of reversals for ERA proponents. President Carter, who supported ERA, proposed registering men and women for the draft. Not just anti-ERA women, but young women who had not taken sides but had benefited from the movement attacked the ERA supporters, blaming them for a policy of subjecting them to involuntary military service in the name of women's equality. In addition, by the end of August 1980, Illinois had refused for the eighth time to ratify the amendment. Then the Republican convention platform repudiated an ERA plank that had existed for forty years as Ronald Reagan was nominated for the presidency. After that, organizers of yet another march could turn out only 500 persons in New York City on August 26, 1980. Then the Democratic convention broke into factions over whether to keep out of the platform a plank denying money and support to any Democratic candidate who was not committed to ERA. The plank was put in after considerable strife.[15]

Disaster followed disaster for ERA proponents. In 1980 Betty Friedan, whose book *The Feminine Mystique* had set the stage for the ERA movement in the 1960s and 1970s, published another book, *The Second Stage*. This time she critically assessed the movement and asked that women's rights proponents turn to restructuring institutions to focus on giving real equality not just to women but also to men and on the desirability of having children. She denounced the first stage as too polarizing. Feminism, or woman's rights advocacy, should be defined as also including men and family. *The Second Stage* came after ERA advocates had already begun to emphasize their support of family rather than permitting the opposition to attack them as antifamily.[16]

Friedan emphasized that women's lack of political power created the necessity for moving to what she called the second stage in order to achieve equality. This emphasis did not immediately seem accurate because there appeared to be more, rather than less public concern about women's political clout. She also insisted that men wanted to change to interdependence rather than maintain traditional roles, but that view was not reflected in the ratification process. In fact, the very opposition to ERA in the states where it had not been ratified was related to a rejection of more change in roles and relationships. Such views may have been present in thirty-five states, or in thirty if we subtract the five that had tried to rescind ERA, but they were not widespread in the others. However, her conclusions had a ring of authority: that if ERA was ever to pass, every organization would have to put aside separate agendas and work together for it; that politicians must see that support for ERA would be a litmus test for their political futures; and that women who had not taken a stand would have to come to understand that their continued opportunities depended on actual support for the equal rights cause. But these views came late in the failing ERA effort. In fact, coming when it did, *The Second Stage* hurt the cause more than it helped, by reinforcing opposition.[17]

Although they were faced with rescissions in Tennessee, Idaho, Kentucky, and Nebraska, a South Dakota attempt to declare void its original ratification because of the extension of the deadline, and the fact that no new states were added in 1981 and 1982, women's groups made one last push to gain ERA. None of the states that attempted rescission had state ERA's. Proponents could no longer count on Republican party support after the repudiation of its long-standing ERA plank in 1980. Republican women like Congresswoman Margaret Heckler of Massachusetts and Helen Milliken, the wife of Michigan's governor, William Milliken, had led the losing fight to get the plank reinserted in the platform although candidate Reagan opposed it. In the final days of battle, past National Republican party Chairwoman Mary Louise Smith of Iowa, who had strongly supported the plank at first, said she felt "comfortable" with the compromise that was achieved. The compromise stated, "We acknowledge the legitimate efforts of those who support or oppose ratification of the Equal Rights Amendment." Essentially, the Phyllis Schlafly-Senator Jesse Helms of North Carolina wing of the party prevailed, keeping the Republicans from continuing their endorsement of ERA.[18]

When ERA opponent Ronald Reagan was elected president, pro-ERA women knew they would get no support from the White House in the final effort to persuade state legislatures. The Nevada Senate rejected the ERA thirty seconds after it was introduced in January 1981. In February 1981, the Virginia House Committee let it die a quiet death without even calling it up for consideration. NOW and

other organizations decided to work hard in 1981 for a last push in
1982. In addition, they supported the introduction, by three Republican senators (Orrin Hatch, Mark Hatfield, and Robert Packwood)
and seventeen House members, of an Economic Equity Act for women
in April 1981. In addition to enhanced child support provisions, the
Act proposed to equalize the treatment of men and women in pensions, insurance, inheritance, child care, and military service. Senator
Hatfield asserted that Reagan had said he supported equality for
women, but not ERA. "Well, OK, here is an alternative" to the ERA.
But as ERA died, much of the Economic Equity Act languished. Over
the next two years consideration of the legislation dragged slowly in
various committees, and much of it failed of passage in the Congress.[19]

In the final stages of the struggle, NOW continued its convention
boycott as a strategy to gain support for the amendment. Missouri,
Nevada, and a tourist group in Louisiana sued in federal court claiming that the boycott violated the Sherman Antitrust Act. The Court
of Appeals for the Eighth Circuit sided with NOW, deciding the Sherman Act did not apply to the use of economic boycotts to influence
social legislation. The Supreme Court denied review, leaving the decision standing. But the boycott strategy did not help very much so
late in the campaign.[20]

In May 1981, NOW sent five teams of missionaries to Utah for the
summer, to knock on doors of Mormons asking them to support ERA.
The Mormon church had officially announced against the amendment. The president of the Mormon church, Spencer Kimball, on
October 22, 1976, had issued a statement that the amendment "would
strike at the family, humankind's basic institution." Increasingly em-
battled, NOW continued to raise money and volunteers for the 1982
push. On June 30, 1981, rallies were held nationwide to support ERA.
Contrary to the front-page publicity of early years, the news was reported in the inside Section B of the *Washington Post*, the *New York
Times*, and other papers.[21]

Then the Supreme Court announced two decisions which did not
help the proponents because one tended toward equality, while the
other did not. In a statutory rape case, the Court ruled that laws which
punish men for the offense but not women were constitutional. Also,
on June 26, 1981, the Court ruled that a military spouse had no right
to share in the ex-soldier's pension after a divorce. Laws had been
recently enacted to give a wife some share of Civil Service and Foreign
Service pensions. But until other changes in law, the Court would give
deference to Congress's power over the control of military affairs, and
pensions were an integral part of a payment system to maintain effective military forces. In both cases, the Court did not challenge the
standard it had utilized since 1976, that a law which distinguished on

the basis of gender must be substantively related to achieving an important government objective. This middle-level standard did not require proof that the legislature had a compelling interest in achieving an objective that was necessary and could not be achieved otherwise, as in race cases. Justice Rehnquist cited all of the familiar precedents upholding the middle-level standard but used instead a "similarly situated" basis for the decision: teenage girls and boys are not similarly situated because only girls can become pregnant. Men and women are not similarly situated because women are barred from combat by certain laws and policies.[22]

Although emphasizing the continuing failure of the Supreme Court to use the same standard in gender discrimination cases as it did in race cases might have fueled support for ERA earlier, the anti campaign was too far advanced. Proponents of ERA had to contend with successes of the anti-ERA forces in the final ratification states and continued complaints that the women's movement was essentially a middle-class, white woman's movement. Opponents emphasized discrimination against black women in the early women's rights movement, the split over suffrage for black men during Reconstruction, and the racism expressed by white women during the suffrage campaigns. Some blacks expressed the view that the movement was designed to achieve white women's gains at the expense of women and men of other races. According to this view, white women would be the major beneficiaries of equal treatment in employment and education. Others noted the emphasis of the women's movement on oppression within the marriage and family, while black women, especially, worried more about discrimination against themselves and black men in the labor force. As Bella Hooks, who called ERA advocates "liberationists," put it,

> When women liberationists emphasized work as a path to liberation, they did not concentrate their attention on those women who are most exploited in the American labor force. . . . While it does not in any way diminish the importance of women resisting sexist oppression by entering the labor force, work has not been a liberating force for masses of American women.[23]

At the Fifth Berkshire Conference on the History of Women in June 1981, Shirlene Soto, California Polytechnic State University historian, noted the importance of race and ethnicity as well as sex. She asserted, "to the Chicano, it makes little difference if she is unemployed because she is a woman or because she is a Chicana." Marquita James of Nassau Community College in Garden City, Long Island, noted that "Black women are almost unanimous in their insistence that their own liberation depends on the liberation of their race."

Eleanor Smith of the University of Cincinnati offered direction for creating sisterhood: white women could examine their roles in contributing to racism, and non-white women could begin to exercise greater activism and leadership on sex and race issues. These criticisms did not help to strengthen the possibility of consensus for ERA's approval in the remaining states.[24]

Even as they digested the Court's decisions and the continuing conflicts and opposition, pro-ERA women kept counting possible states for ratification and included Florida as a real possibility. But Dempsey Barron, the Senate Rules Committee chairman with strong ties to the insurance industry, kept saying "I'm personally strongly opposed to the ERA." In 1979 he used parliamentary tactics to kill the bill 21–19, and as for the last session before the 1982 deadline, he announced in July 1981, "It's a moot issue. It's dead." He bragged about his sole responsibility for killing the amendment. Every year since 1972 the legislature either refused to consider it or failed to ratify. "Women don't need any more help," Barron stated. "They've already got 50 percent of the money and 100 percent of the other things men need."[25]

A Gallup poll reported, in August 1981, that 63 percent of the Americans who had heard about it supported ERA, a higher percentage than in any poll before. But Gallup predicted ratification would be difficult. Opposition was still great among Republicans, people living in the Midwest and the South, and among older Americans.

The positive poll results were really negative because additional ratifications needed to come from the states in which support was identified as weakest. Not conceding the issue, on August 22, 1981, NOW held another rally and walk-a-thon to raise funds and motivate supporters in cities across the country. Former First Lady Betty Ford, Maureen Reagan, daughter of the president, and other notables marched and raised funds. The walk-a-thon attracted crowds of mainly young, white women, some of whom wheeled babies in carriages. Esther Rolle, the star of the TV show "Good Times" was one of the prominent black women participants. She commented that many black women feel they "still have a job to do" to achieve just racial equality. Ellie Smeal, in the last year of her term as NOW president, was optimistic, still targeting Florida, Illinois, Missouri, Oklahoma, North Carolina, Virginia, and Georgia as the states in which she sensed ratification had the best chance for approval.[26]

In the state election in Virginia, pro-ERA forces picked up three votes in November 1981. In Florida, in two special elections, they got a seat in the House and one in the Senate. At its convention in October, NOW announced a $15 million advertising drive for ERA, and an ERA message brigade to enroll one million supporters who, upon receiving alerts that action was needed in unratified states, would send messages to key political leaders in those states. In addition, the group announced an expansion to other states of the Utah door-to-door missionary project, and an ERA impact project in the sixteen states with state provisions to show that rights of men and women improved. On October 12, 1981, NOW organized another series of rallies with former First Ladies Betty Ford and Lady Bird Johnson leading the notables.[27]

By January 1982, the supporters clearly were almost at the end of their rope. The Utah legislature adjourned on January 31. The Virginia legislature was supposed to adjourn on March 13, and Florida on March 18. Georgia had a possible adjournment date of February 18, and legislatures in four other unratified states would adjourn by the end of April.[28] A group of nine ERA supporters chained themselves to the main gate of the Mormon Temple in Kensington, Maryland, on January 9, 1982, in protest against the upholding of rescissions by Judge Callister, who was a leader in the Mormon church. They were led by Sonia Johnson, a president of Mormons for ERA, who was excommunicated from the church in 1979 for her pro-ERA activities. Johnson did not chain herself to the fence but led protest songs and carried a sign saying, "Bigots make bad missionaries."[29]

On January 12, 1982, a Georgia House Committee voted 6-3 to send ERA to the floor with a favorable recommendation. But the bill, defeated in 1974 and 1980, was not given a good chance for passage. In Oklahoma the Senate voted against ratification on January 13, but a state senator introduced a motion for reconsideration. In Illinois the governor called for ratification in his State of the State address, but the legislature adjourned until March. Former Presidents Carter and Ford issued a joint call on January 18, for ratification. In Virginia on January 18, the House Speaker, A.L. Phillpott gave ERA opponents a majority on a critical legislative committee which had to consider the bill. On January 19, on reconsideration, the Oklahoma Senate voted 27–21 to reject it. The Georgia House killed it by a 2–1 margin on January 20, 1981, despite pleas from black and feminist lawmakers and Presidents Carter and Ford and their wives. The Catholic bishop of Richmond issued a strong endorsement for ratification on January 22, 1982. He stated, "I do not fear the consequences of ERA so much as I fear for the many women who will continue to suffer blatant injustices and oppression without ERA."[30]

By January 25, 1982, when the Supreme Court took itself out of the debate over extension and ratification by issuing a stay of Judge Callister's December 1981 decision in *Idaho* v. *Freeman* until it could decide the issues, failure was increasingly imminent. NOW tried to defeat the opposition by pointing out that Judge Callister, because of

his Mormon church leadership, had been asked to remove himself
from the case and refused. Smeal declared his decision in the case
"outrageous," but Ruth Hinerfeld, president of the League of Women
Voters, asserted, "We knew we had an uphill battle before the decision—but we were really thinking things were looking up." She
thought "legislators will seize on this decision as an excuse for inaction." Phyllis Schlafly, on the other hand, kept reminding people of
the decision and of what a "great victory" it was for her side. Senate
Democratic whip Alan Cranston, a leader in the fight for extension,
agreed with Schlafly. He thought the decision made ratification "impossible unless something changes."[31]

The Reagan administration had joined the *Idaho* case debate on the
side of NOW asking that the ruling be immediately nullified. Some
administration officials worried that the gender gap be might be a
force in the 1984 election and, believing the amendment would be
defeated anyway, thought they would lose nothing by arguing against
the decision on the technical grounds of congressional control of ratification. In any case, they assumed that the Court was unlikely to
overrule precedent on the political question issue. None of the parties
had asked for a stay, but opponents and proponents knew that under
tradition the Court does not issue a stay unless it believes the appealing
party has a strong likelihood of prevailing on the merits. However,
ratification appeared more and more unlikely and the controversy
helped to fuel the continuing opposition.[32]

In Virginia, on February 1, the House killed an effort to bypass the
ERA opponent-dominated Committee on Privileges and Elections to
bring ERA directly to the floor. The vote was 62–35 without discussion. The committee killed the bill 12–7 on February 3. ERA failed
in the Senate by a vote of 20–19 on February 16, 1982. Republican
state Senator Nathan H. Miller, one opponent of the bill, remained
absent to prevent a 20–20 vote which could have been untied by an
affirmative vote of supporter, Democratic Lieutenant Governor Richard J. Davis. Miller prevented the bill from obtaining the constitutional
majority required for approval. On February 2, 1983, NOW announced the end of its boycott of Miami Beach, whose state delegation
had consistently voted 100% for ERA.[33]

Still not conceding defeat, in late May, ERA backers claimed they
might achieve a surprise victory in North Carolina where Governor
Hunt strongly supported them and a statewide poll showed 2–1 support. Grassroots support continued as donations to NOW reached
about $1 million a month, triple the previous year's figures. In ad-
dition, seven women in Illinois pursued a hunger strike into its tenth
day in an effort to aid passage. On June 3, seventeen supporters of
the amendment calling themselves a Grass Roots Group of Second

Class Citizens chained themselves to the Illinois Senate chamber. The seven fasters left, in order to separate themselves from the chainees, but vowed to continue the fast. In North Carolina on June 4, the Senate voted 27–23 in support of a table motion on the bill. About 4,000 persons, including pros and antis, lobbied the legislature on the day before the vote. Antis won since no action was taken. But, Florida Governor Bob Graham called a special session of the legislature for June 21 to consider the amendment.[34]

Matters worsened in Illinois. State police with chain cutters surprised the chained women at the Illinois Senate rail at 4 A.M. on June 7. They refused to move and were dragged away but not arrested. The fasters, including Sonia Johnson, who was hospitalized briefly, continued their 21st day of the fast. Governor Thompson announced that "the chains haven't helped, the fasters haven't helped, the marchers haven't helped, the picketers haven't helped." Republican state Senator Forest D. Etheredge said he would not vote on the amendment until the fast ended. House Speaker George Ryan, Thompson's running mate, when asked about the marchers, said, "Why should I want to watch those idiots?" Anti-ERA women gathered to eat candy bars in front of the fasters. One held a sign saying "Are you for ERA? Evil, Rebellious, Agitators, the Communists, lesbians, and homosexuals, and those who work to destroy America and the right to be a true wife and homebuilder are for the ERA."[35]

On June 22, the Illinois House voted 103–72, four votes short of the 107 needed for a three-fifths majority of ERA. In Florida, on June 21, the special session voted in the Senate 22–16 against the amendment. In Oklahoma, Governor Nigh said he would not call the legislature into a special session unless two more states ratified. The Florida action left Illinois as the only possibility left. A new poll showed that 62 percent of the people in Illinois supported the amendment on June 14, but on June 24 the Illinois House rejected the amendment for the seventh time. On that day, Eleanor Smeal acknowledged defeat but vowed to continue the struggle. NOW would continue to try to elect state legislators and sue corporations whom Smeal believed had funded the opposition. "We've just begun to fight," she said. But Phyllis Schlafly gleefully predicted ERA would "take its place with the prohibition and child labor amendments as ones which did not have enough support of the American people to be in the Constitution."[36]

In the aftermath of ERA's defeat, proponents began to assess the reasons for failure. Gloria Steinem judged that the movement did not focus single-mindedly on ERA until too late. Eleanor Smeal did not disagree, but conceded that she may have spent too much time on details before embarking on new tactics. Steinem thought the boycott of unratified states should have started sooner. One tactic that was started late was a campaign against insurance companies which Smeal contended wanted to maintain discriminatory rates for women. Smeal also pinpointed too late the most obvious reason for the failure. She blamed complacency in the movement after Congress approved the amendment: "The movement never realized the depth of the opposition." For the future, she projected focusing on the fact that 75 percent of the female legislators in the states that did not ratify, as opposed to 45 percent of the men, supported ERA. This meant an organizational emphasis on increasing the numbers of women legislators. Some analysts blamed defeat on the leadership style of ERA supporters, lesbians, radicals, and the like. Others blamed the convention boycotts which some civil libertarians regard as unfair. Others cited attacks on traditional female roles—abortion, child care and undermining the family. Others cited a confusion of goals—a failure to be clear about whether it was gender neutrality or a special status for women the supporters wanted. Although 52 percent of women worked outside their homes in 1982, compared to 39 percent in 1965, arguments against ERA seemed still to assume most women were housewives—they may have wanted to be, but they were not.[37]

Phyllis Schlafly opined that she had seen the end of ERA, announcing that her 50,000 member organization could turn to a campaign against sex education as a principal cure of teenage pregnancy, and a campaign against a nuclear freeze ("The atomic bomb is a marvelous gift that was given to our country by a wise God."). In addition, they would mount an effort to rid school texts of feminist influence ("The way it is now, you can't show a picture of a woman washing the dishes.").[38]

The supporters of ERA in Congress led by Patricia Schroeder (D, Colo.), Don Edwards (D, Calif.), and Speaker Thomas P. (Tip) O'Neill (D, Mass.) did not give up the effort either. They announced on July 14, that they had fifty-one cosponsors in the Senate and 201 in the House to reintroduce ERA. However, Senate Majority Leader Howard Baker (R, Tenn.) said he advocated "a little cooling off" and Assistant Majority Leader Ted Stevens (R, Alaska) said he did not expect Congress to act unless prodded by state legislatures. Although time ran out in the congressional session and by January the Republicans had gained control of the Senate with a hostile Senator Orrin Hatch of Utah as chairman of the key committee involved, the first House Resolution of the year was ERA. But even as the renewed battle for ERA geared up, assessments continued on what went wrong before.[39]

The ERA was passed in the House in 1972 during a period of confrontation with authority over the Vietnam war. Significantly, just as the failed child labor amendment came as the Progressive movement was over, ERA came from a Democratically controlled Congress at the tail end of the civil rights and war on poverty movements of the 1960's. Whether it was the insurance companies or other corporate interests, or the financial power of the Mormon church, arguments against the amendment were enough to persuade many women and men to oppose ERA in the final states needed for ratification. These in turn convinced many legislators that they had nothing to lose politically by voting against ERA and much to gain. In other words, enough voters in their districts were against ERA or lukewarm so that they did not risk retribution in voting against it. If they were personally for it, they would run great risks by voting in the affirmative. Opinion already existed or was shaped in thirteen states to defeat the amendment.[40]

The absence of supportive consensus for ERA reflected fundamental opposition to changing the traditional roles women and men play. Even if women were known to be outside-the-home workers, this was not regarded as their major priority. Also, something fundamental about being a woman and a man seemed threatened—woman's place, man's place, child's place as the ideal even when not the reality.

The mere possibility, without a probable reality, of sex integrated washrooms and prisons, or the loss of legal preferences for married women was enough to threaten the traditionalists. In short, beyond equal pay for equal work, which was already provided for by Title VII of the Civil Rights Act of 1964 and the Equal Pay Act, many people did not want women to be equal to men. In some cases they wanted women to be better off—more advantaged than men and in other ways subordinated. As Phyllis Schlafly put it, "ERA was the men's liberation amendment." It would give men more freedom to abandon responsibilities without giving women any valuable rights in return. The only way polls could be taken to dispute this notion was to ask, not whether people were for or against ERA, but were they for or against any consequences of ERA that anti-ERA women could project. Even then polls gave no useful answer unless they also asked, do you know that ERA cannot be passed unless three-fourths of the states pass it and do you insist that your state legislator vote for it? Otherwise some people might say they were for it because they thought it would not happen, and they did not want to tell a poll taker that they were opposed to equality for someone. Some might say they were for it because they believed it would do something that was not at all in the poll taker's thoughts. Others might say they were against it for similar reasons. These reasons might have been more effectively expressed to their legislators than to the pollsters.[41]

To argue that women were already in the military offered no answer to anti-ERA women, who either thought they should not be, or that,

if they were, they should expect to be treated differently from men
as punishment for doing what they should not do. To argue that the
abortion issue was irrelevant because abortion was already legal was
no answer to those who hoped the Supreme Court would one day
outlaw it and who thought pro-choice was a code word for women
wanting to escape the biological functions that made them women, in
order to be like men. To argue that Congress would not automatically
have to fund abortions after ERA was no answer to those who wanted
to be absolutely sure that Congress never could fund them. In a sense,
being forced to bear an unwanted child was, to them, being forced
to accept that one was a woman and different from men. Arguing
that the right to privacy would prevent sex integration of restrooms
was no answer to people who were not constitutional lawyers and who
asked only, why does the amendment say equality of the sexes shall
not be abridged if that is not what it means?

The ratification struggle came to an end as assessments of supporters and opponents did not change much from the period before
the extension of time for adoption of the amendment. Amendment
opponents were more religious, a little older, and somewhat less educated, though middle-class. They were more likely to belong to the
John Birch Society, the Eagle Forum, or the DAR, although there
were homemakers for ERA and people of faith for ERA. Arguing
that the amendment would help working women and was not antifamily did not help with women who liked the idea of father as head,
mother as nurturer and manager, and children as extensions of the
family into the future. Father was not wanted as nurturer and manager in the family, and those women did not want to be thought of
as providers, except as anomalies. They most certainly did not want
their children to be cared for in day care facilities where they might
become the objects of child abuse at worst and at best develop different
belief systems from their parents.

Although anti-ratificationists utilized sophisticated direct mail techniques and were led by a very experienced professional, Phyllis
Schlafly, they managed to remain identified as grassroots housewives
and homemakers unmotivated by any broad political purposes. When
the first twenty-two states ratified quickly, no debate had taken place
or was considered necessary. But as soon as Schlafly and her supporters took the offensive, ERA backers, unprepared for the on-
slaught, found themselves having to explain not only to legislators,
but to women, why they were trying to undermine women.

The debates highlighted the essential vulnerability some women felt
about their social situation. In this view, female solidarity in the notion
that men were constrained by traditional rules to give women a modi-
cum of decency and respect, which might or might not be equitable,

had protected women. Moving to something called equality seemed too threatening to that vulnerability. Unchartered waters, the unknown, could unleash forces that, while spoken of in terms of equality, would make many women more vulnerable and exposed. Better to remain with the known, which at least was clear and understood. Women's rights proponents, in this sense, could be seen as doing women wrong by shattering female solidarity, putting all women at risk.

Called into question at the time ERA was before the states for ratification was a whole panoply of cultural shocks and changes related to equality. Changes in race relations and sexual mores, all were called into question. Governmental actions required to implement equality—school desegregation, busing, affirmative action—all became controversial and threatening to some people. Equality may have seemed simple to proratificationists, but to others it meant sexual permissiveness, the pill, abortion, living in communes, draft dodger, unisex men who refused to be men, and women who refused to be women. It meant women who did not believe they could or should compete with men having to do so just because some unusual women could or wanted to. It also represented fear that men would feel freer to abandon family responsibilities and nothing would be gained in exchange. These issues arose during the debates in the unratified states and rescission states and had not been sufficiently debated in those that had ratified early.

Few of these concerns seemed to penetrate the consciousness of those who immediately determined to reintroduce the amendment. Indeed, throughout the whole period before the reintroduction of the amendment in January 1983, supporters discounted these issues, dismissing them as irrelevant "horribles." They were, in the sense they meant it, irrelevant to the principle of according to women equality of rights in a democracy under the Constitution. But the antiratificationists had succeeded in drawing attention away from the constitutional principle, to traditional family values and roles as the turf on which the battle was fought. The proponents seemed to have no consistent strategy for restoring the balance necessary for stimulating the development of increasing consensus in the Congress and the states.

Legal Developments in the Courts and in the States: The Brooding Omnipresence of ERA

8

Despite its failure, the campaign for ERA's ratification stimulated significant alteration in the legal status of women. Brown, Emerson, Falk, and Freedmen in the influential 1971 *Yale Law Review* article widely used in the congressional debates preceding the passage of ERA, predicted that "any present hope for large-scale change can hardly be deemed realistic" if one relied on the courts to guarantee equality for women under the Fourteenth Amendment. Although it is true that courts did not guarantee equality, between 1972 and 1982 the Supreme Court gradually broadened protection for women under the Fourteenth Amendment equal protection clause. The Court also interpreted broadly the provisions of the 1963 amendment to the Fair Labor Standards Act requiring equal pay for equal work between men and women, and Title VII of the Civil Rights Act of 1964 outlawing sex discrimination by employers of more than fifteen persons. In addition to Supreme Court action, several states adopted state ERA's during the same period, although some had been adopted previously. However, little guidance as to whether ERA would be ratified could be gained from the existence of a state ERA without analyzing its uses by a state's courts and legislature.[1]

In 1971 while the ERA was before the Congress, the Supreme Court had upheld an Idaho woman's claim that a state court's appointment of her estranged husband as administrator of her deceased child's estate under state law which favored men as administrators, violated the equal protection clause of the Fourteenth Amendment.[2] In 1973, the Court found a federal law distinguishing between women and men unconstitutional as a violation of equal protection implicit in the Fifth Amendment. The law automatically made dependents of male military personnel eligible for a basic subsistence allowance but made dependents of female military personnel prove actual dependency.[3] The Court also declared unconstitutional under the Fourteenth

Amendment a Utah law that required divorced fathers to support their sons to age twenty-one but their daughters only to age eighteen;[4] an Oklahoma law that permitted the sale of beer to women at age eighteen but to men only at age twenty-one;[5] and a Louisiana law that excluded women from jury duty unless they were volunteers.[6]

In the employment area, in 1971 the Court decided that refusing to hire women, but not men, with preschool age children violated Title VII of the Civil Rights Act of 1964.[7] Also the Court found that paying women day workers less, as a minimum wage, than men night shift workers when both performed the same tasks, violated the Equal Pay Act of 1963.[8] The Court also decided that an Alabama law that stipulated minimum height and weight requirements for prison guards illegally excluded women from these jobs in violation of Title VII of the Civil Rights Act of 1964.[9]

In addition, the Supreme Court decided that states could not force women to take maternity leave at a specific time, but that employers could deny disability benefits to women undergoing normal pregnancy.[10] Congress responded by enacting the Pregnancy Discrimination Act of 1978 to make clear that the benefits should be provided.[11] The Court also found that Social Security programs could not provide benefits to widows that they did not give to widowers.[12] The overall effect of these decisions was to provide for more equal treatment between women and men under the law.

After ERA had been voted out of the Congress and was in the state ratification process in 1978, the Supreme Court decided a number of cases which took a less expansive view of women's legal equality. One decision announced that Title VII prohibits an employer from requiring women to make larger contributions in order to get the same monthly pensions as men.[13] But the Court refused to accept the doctrine that government classification by gender must be regarded as inherently suspect, requiring a state to prove a compelling interest to pass the challenged law because there was no other way to achieve a necessary result. This doctrine, which lawyers refer to as "strict scrutiny," requires such a standard when race classification is enacted into law. However, the Court did go so far as to move beyond the previously used "rational basis" test, which required only that the legislation be reasonable, not arbitrary, and have a fair and substantial relation to the object of the legislation. The Court majority adopted a "modified rational basis" test. This test required that the classification "must serve important governmental objectives and must be substantially related to the achievement of those objectives." The importance of these doctrines is that they define how much a person who challenged the law in question had to prove and what arguments were acceptable in defense.[14]

The Court's refusal to adopt a "strict scrutiny" test permitted it to uphold a number of laws that would have been declared unconstitutional if they had involved discrimination by race. In 1975, a state law exempting widows from a special property tax in 1974 and a federal law that gave women reserve officers a longer period than men in which to seek promotion gained approval.[15] Also, the Court upheld a state law charging a male with statutory rape for having sex with a female under eighteen but not a woman who had sex with a male under age eighteen.[16] In short, the Court still recognized certain differences between men and women and indicated a clear ideological position permitting the recognition of these differences in law.

The Court also refused to accept the doctrine that practices which appear to be neutral, but which have a disproportionate negative impact on one sex only, should be subjected to "strict scrutiny" and struck down on the basis of disparate impact. For example, in 1979, the Court refused to reject a Massachusetts veterans' preference law that resulted in the total exclusion of women from the upper echelons of the state civil service. The Court rationalized that the law seemed to treat all veterans equally, even though women had less opportunity to be veterans, given the restricted opportunities for military service, so to gain preferences.[17] If the proponents of ERA still believed that the protections the Court refused to give were necessary in these cases, they still needed an ERA. In 1973, Justice Powell specifically mentioned the absence of an ERA as a reason *not* to treat sex classification as "suspect," saying that ratification would "resolve the substance of this precise question." Essentially, the Court asserted that women who wanted ERA did not need ERA because they had the Fourteenth Amendment; but they were also being told they could not have "strict scrutiny" under the Fourteenth Amendment unless they did have ERA.[18]

The legality of abortion as an option for pregnant women was affirmed by the Court during this same period, but the decision did not keep opponents from arguing throughout the ratification campaign that an ERA would enshrine abortion as a constitutional right. Proponents, many of whom favored legal abortion, found themselves having to argue the issue with legislators and opponents who either did not understand the legal irrelevancy or pretended they did not. Phyllis Schlafly in her *Reports* and public appearances constantly linked the amendment to abortion. In heavily Catholic Illinois the argument was particularly effective.[19]

The Supreme Court, in *Roe* v. *Wade* in 1973, struck down a Texas law that made abortion a criminal offense, on the ground that the law violated a woman's constitutional right of privacy under the Fourteenth Amendment. Justice Blackmun's majority opinion stated that in the first and second trimester of pregnancy a woman had the right, with her physician, to choose, and the state's power was subordinate to their decision. In the third trimester the state could prohibit abortion, but not if it was needed to save the life or health of the mother. In *Doe* v. *Bolton* in 1973, the Court used the same doctrine to void a Georgia law that made abortion criminal and had unnecessary medical exceptions.[20]

The Court upheld, however, the right of states to refuse to pay the cost of non-therapeutic abortions. In *Maher* v. *Doe* in 1977, the Court decided that it was not a denial of equal protection of the laws for Connecticut to deny public funding for Medicaid recipients' abortions. In *Harris* v. *McRae*, the Court upheld a federal law enacted in 1976, called the Hyde amendment, in response to *Roe* v. *Wade*, that prohibited Medicaid funding for abortions that were not medically necessary. Essentially, women had a right to abortion, but funding for health care for poor women could not be used for their abortions. In 1983, in a series of cases, the Court reaffirmed *Roe* v. *Wade* and its progeny. Efforts continued in the Congress to gain a constitutional amendment to outlaw abortion, and opponents of the Equal Rights Amendment continued to argue that it would permit abortion, although abortion was already permitted. They also argued ERA would change the Court's posture on funding of abortions for poor women. However, the Court in *Harris* v. *McRae* decided that the protection of a right from governmental interference did not imply governmental responsibility to pay for the right involved. Nothing in the opinion decided that an equal rights for women amendment would convert a non-right to payment into a right to payment. But this fact did not dampen the discussions of abortion in the ratification campaigns.[21]

Opponents also continued to argue that an ERA would legalize homosexual marriages, despite court decisions to the contrary. In *Baker* v. *Nelson*, the Supreme Court of Minnesota in 1971 decided that the right to marry without regard to sex is not a fundamental right compelled by the federal Constitution. No reported cases had been decided differently. In the hearings on the Equal Rights Amendment in the Congress the issue was raised again and again, although the proponents of the amendment affirmed the view of the cases that prohibiting discrimination on the basis of sex did not mean or imply prohibiting discrimination on the basis of sexual preference. In other words, if a state decided to legalize marriages between men and men, it would be required to legalize marriages between women and women, or vice versa. But otherwise the amendment would have no effect on legalizing sexual preference. What was overlooked continuously in the interjection of such issues as abortion and homosexuality into the debates, was the fact that the Equal Rights Amendment, like the equal protection clause of the Fourteenth Amendment, had nothing to do with private conduct but covered only actions by government.[22]

Although opponents kept raising it as an argument against ERA, the issue of women and the draft was settled by the Supreme Court in 1981. Essentially, with or without the Equal Rights Amendment, Congress could decide under its powers to make rules concerning the military—either to draft women or not. Congress could also, with or without an ERA, assign women to combat and other tasks, so long as they based assignments on individual abilities to perform and not on the fact that a person was a woman or a man. Even with ERA, the Congress would be required to do no more or less.[23]

In addition to the statutes and case law on women's rights in the courts, several states passed equal rights amendments and laws during the unsuccessful struggle to ratify ERA. However, three of the states (Illinois, Virginia, and Utah) that did not ratify ERA had state provisions in their own constitutions. Nine of the states that ratified ERA (Colorado, Hawaii, Maryland, Massachusetts, New Hampshire, New Mexico, Pennsylvania, Texas, and Washington) had provisions that read the same or about the same as the federal provision. They prohibited the states from abridging equality of rights on account of sex.

Illinois, which did not ratify ERA, had adopted a new constitution in 1970 which included in the Bill of Rights an equal rights provision which states: "The equal protection of the laws shall not be denied or abridged on account of sex by the state or its units of local government and school districts."

A closer look at the Illinois experience supports the view that the arguments made by federal ERA opponents in that state, as in others with equal rights amendments, could be made validly only about matters under federal control, such as military service. This was because any issues involving state action were already controlled by the state ERA. Phyllis Schlafly, who began her anti-ERA campaign in Illinois only because Alton, Illinois was her home, said she supported Illinois's state ERA. She viewed it, as did Senator Sam J. Ervin, Jr., of North Carolina, as permitting fair and reasonable distinctions on the basis of gender, unlike the federal ERA which uses "equality of rights" language. This argument is specious because the Illinois ERA was interpreted by that state's supreme court in *People* v. *Ellis* to make sex a "suspect" classification, and, therefore, subjected sex-based distinctions to "strict scrutiny" and not to a test of fairness or reasonableness.[24]

In Illinois family law on custody issues, the best interest of the child continued to be the operable theory with no presumption that the mother had a superior custody right. In *Marcus* v. *Marcus* in 1975, the appellate court stated that: "The fact that a mother is fit is only one facet of the situation, and, standing for itself, it does not authorize a denial of custody to the father, when this appears necessary because of other considerations."[25] But the courts held that the state ERA permits, in some cases, the presumption that custody of children of tender age be given to the mother, as one of several factors considered flexibly in determining child custody cases.[26] In *Atkinson* v. *Atkinson* in 1980, the Illinois appellate court found that despite the state ERA, a trial court could consider the sex of the children as one factor in custody cases.[27]

On the issue of marriage licenses, Illinois adopted strict equality of treatment for males and females. In *Phelps* v. *Bing* in 1974, the Illinois Supreme Court invalidated a state law that provided different age limits by gender. The law had provided that a female could obtain a marriage license without parental consent at age eighteen, with parental consent at sixteen, and at fifteen by court order; while a male had to be twenty-one to marry without parental consent, eighteen to marry with consent, and sixteen to marry by court order.[28]

On married women's names, the attorney general of Illinois issued an opinion in February 1974, that because of ERA women could keep and use their own names just as men did. In addition, in a 1976 case the Illinois Supreme Court held that the doctrine of "interspousal immunity," barring personal injury suits between spouses, did not violate the state ERA because its provisions apply equally to men and women.[29]

In athletics, the state appellate court found in *Petrie* v. *Illinois High School Association* that the Illinois ERA did not prohibit a state high school athletic conference from refusing to permit boys to play on the all-girl volleyball team when there was no compelling state interest in fostering interscholastic athletic competition. The dissent objected that this result was an example of attempting to protect females because they are classified as weak and inferior. The court did not decide what would happen if there were both boys' and girls' volleyball teams and either a boy or girl was prohibited from choosing to try out for either.[30]

When Karren O'Connor, an exceptionally talented eleven-year-old female basketball player, was refused a try-out on the boys' team, she attempted to gain an injunction against the policy under the Fourteenth Amendment, the Fifth Amendment, and the state ERA. The lower court granted an injunction. However, she lost in the appellate court which found the trial court had analyzed the federal claim without using the "rational basis" standard, which required only that the law be substantially related to a legitimate governmental interest. The appellate court, citing *Petrie*, discounted the claim under the Illinois ERA. The U.S. Supreme Court denied an appeal. The case was sent back for a trial on the merits.[31]

Consistently using the "strict scrutiny" standard in analyzing its Equal Rights Amendment regarding pensions, the state upheld the equal rights of dependent husbands and wives to receive accidental death benefits under the state retirement system. Also, in *People* v. *Ellis*, Illinois courts invalidated a juvenile justice provision for differential treatment if girls were under eighteen or if boys were under seventeen. Using "strict scrutiny" as the standard again, the court decided the same age had to be used for both.[32]

In two kinds of cases, males accused of criminal behavior attempted to use the ERA to gain acquittal. The physical difference that permits women, but not men, to become pregnant helped to decide the issues. A father lost an appeal of his incest conviction based on the fact that a mother who committed incest with a son received a lesser penalty by statute than a father who committed incest with a daughter. The court analyzed the case based on the identification of the culprit, deciding that the probability of pregnancy of the person on whom the incest was inflicted justified a harsher penalty.[33] In 1974 the appellate court held that the state rape statute, under which only men could be convicted of the crime, was not made unconstitutional by virtue of the ERA. The court found that even under the "strict scrutiny" test there was a compelling state interest in seeing to it that men did not rape women who could become pregnant. However, the court noted that a woman could be guilty of rape of a woman, as an accessory, an aider, or abettor of the male rapist.[34]

A similar result was reached in a 1979 case when a man objected to the revocation of his prohibition from a conviction for pandering, on the ground that the statute which made it a crime to compel a woman, but not a man, to become a prostitute was unconstitutional. The court held that the man could not challenge the law because men and women alike could be convicted of the crime of enticing a female to be a prostitute. Furthermore, the court stated, he would have lost because even under "strict scrutiny" the state could show a compelling interest in protecting women, who could become pregnant, from prostitution while choosing not to protect men.[35]

In another case in 1979, the court decided that a statute which prohibited a person of one sex from performing a massage on an individual of the other sex was unconstitutional under the state ERA. The state could not, under the "strict scrutiny" doctrine, show that the classification was necessary to prevent obscene conduct. The court asserted that either sex could engage in obscene conduct and if the state's objective was to outlaw such behavior, the law did not need to discriminate on the basis of sex.[36]

While ERA was before the states for ratification, the Illinois courts in general had held that the state's ERA did not invalidate laws based on biological differences between women and men. "Strict scrutiny" had been uniformly applied, but so long as similarly situated males and females were treated identically, there was no issue of classification based on sex. In addition, the state ERA was held to operate prospectively, so that any conduct that occurred before its adoption could not be challenged under its provisions.

In addition to court cases, the Illinois state legislature amended provisions of the state code to bring them into conformity with the state ERA. Such matters as discrimination in credit cards, admission to public schools, physical education classes, and interscholastic athletics were all the subject of statutory changes. In addition, the legislature in July 1980 enacted a broad Human Rights Act barring discrimination between women and men in employment, real estate transactions, access to financial credit, and public accommodations.[37]

In sum, in Illinois under the state ERA everything that could be done under state constitutional control which could equalize the status of men and women was being done. But Illinois had one of the most protracted struggles, led by Phyllis Schlafly and based on fears about matters controlled by the national government, to prevent the ratification of the federal ERA. Other than the strategy of attempting to obtain the election of proratification legislators, the proponents of ERA in Illinois needed to find ways to persuade more legislators and their constituents that issues beyond state control, such as military service and abortion, would also be resolved under a federal ERA in ways that would not be harmful to men, women, children, or families. They did not make the case in time for ratification to occur.

In Utah, one of the three states with state ERAs that did not ratify the Equal Rights Amendment, women's rights had come early. The Mormon church supported woman suffrage in territorial days, but since there were as many women as men in the new state, they would have voted it down. At the same time and for the same reasons, to blunt arguments that women were treated unfairly under polygamy, the state constitution of 1896 stated: "The rights of citizens of the State of Utah to vote and hold office shall not be denied or abridged on account of sex. Both male and female citizens of the State shall enjoy equally all civil, political, and religious rights and privileges."[38]

The provision, unlike the federal ERA, covers public and private conduct. But in 1933 the same constitution expressly authorized the establishment of a minimum wage for women and children only.[39] It also prohibited children under fourteen and women from working in underground mines, until 1980 when the clause excluding women was abolished.[40]

During the period of the ratification struggle, in addition to the clear evidence in the constitution itself that the rights granted women were purposefully limited, the Utah Supreme Court never invalidated a statute based on ERA. Routinely, consistent with their understanding that the state ERA served a narrow political purpose at the time and was really a sham, the state's highest court used a "rational basis" test, requiring only that legislation be reasonable and related to the legislative purpose in cases brought under the state ERA. By emphasizing traditional husband-wife relations and biological factors, the court reduced the state ERA to a nullity. In family law cases, the Utah court continued to assert that women should care for and have custody of children, especially in their earliest years.[41] It upheld different ages of majority for men and women only to be reversed by the U.S. Supreme Court.[42] It also upheld gender distinctions in state laws covering wills, based on the duty of the husband to support the wife.[43] Furthermore, in employment cases, the Utah Supreme Court rejected a female police officer's argument that paying her less than male police officers performing the same work and with the same degree of competency violated the state ERA. The court took into account not only seniority, but other "factors."[44]

The Utah Supreme Court also rejected a pregnant woman's claim that a law declaring a pregnant individual ineligible for unemployment insurance for twelve weeks prior to and six weeks after childbirth was illegal under the state ERA. The woman was involuntarily separated for reasons unrelated to pregnancy and wanted to collect unemployment compensation. The court accepted that view on the grounds that it would be equally applicable to men, if they could become pregnant, and stated, "What she should do is work for the repeal of the biological law of nature. . . . In the matter of pregnancy there is no way to find equality between men and women." The U.S. Supreme Court vacated the judgment, holding that the conclusive presumption that all women could not work at any job when pregnant violated the due process clause of the Fourteenth Amendment.[45]

In addition to the Utah court's disdain for the ERA, the state legislature undertook no comprehensive statutory review to gender neutralize the state code. Essentially, in Utah opponents of ERA could make all of the same arguments about the impact on families, employment, and the like that could be made in states that did not have ERAs, since their own state ERA was well understood as purposely having little impact. They could, in addition, raise the same issues raised in Illinois concerning abortion and military service.

Virginia, the third state with an ERA in its constitution that did not ratify the federal ERA, provides another instructive example of the barriers to ratification. The state provision in the due process clause of the constitution states: "The right to be free from any governmental discrimination upon the basis of religious conviction, race, color, sex, or national origin shall not be abridged, except that mere separation of the sexes shall not be considered discrimination."[46]

Two differences from the proposed federal ERA were obvious: sex was in the same category, with the same legal rules to be applied, as other discrimination, and unlike the Utah ERA, private conduct was not covered; second, unlike the federal amendment and all other state ERAs, Virginia's provision expressly states that "mere separation of the sexes" is not a violation. This language, apparently directed at "unisex" toilets and prisons, could, of course, reduce the general effect of the ERA on the ground that any classification is merely permissible separation of the sexes.[47]

Furthermore, the Virginia Supreme Court adopted a "rational basis" standard for analyzing cases under the state ERA, even though race and sex discrimination are both forbidden in its language. It can be argued that the court should have adopted a "strict scrutiny" standard, since under a U.S. Supreme Court analysis, such cases require such a standard. It could also be argued that the court should have used a "modified rational basis" standard requiring more justification, as the U.S. Supreme Court has since 1976 in sex discrimination cases. But it had done neither.[48] The Virginia Supreme Court, in deciding a 1973 case challenging its use of the "rational basis" test in upholding the statute's sex-based classification, decided that the state ERA is "no broader than the Equal Protection Clause of the Fourteenth Amendment . . . where a statute is based on a reasonable classification that bears a rational relationship to the objective of the state . . . there is no impermissible discrimination under the Constitution of Virginia."[49] The result is that in Virginia courts women have a harder time winning a case under the state ERA than they would under the equal protection clause of the Fourteenth Amendment.

Before the defeat of the federal ERA, the Virginia legislature had acted to eliminate some instances of sex bias in the state code. Spouses were required to support each other and their children. There was no legal bar to support and maintenance for a husband when he was dependent. Women and men had the same grounds for annulment and divorce, and strong fair credit and housing provisions and prohibitions against sex discrimination in automobile insurance had been enacted. However, the husband was still presumed to be the owner of all real property that his wife possessed during the marriage, unless the woman could introduce facts to prove the husband gave up the

ownership. Only women could be rape victims and only men per-
petrators of rape and seduction. Illegitimate children could inherit
from their mothers in all circumstances, but from their intestate fathers only if the father had taken a series of elaborate steps to establish
paternity.[50]

In general, Virginia's ERA had less effect on the legal rights of
women than use of the Fourteenth Amendment equal protection
clause by itself would have had. Statutes that could be declared illegal
under the state ERA remained in force, and court decisions limited
the amendment's impact. Essentially, opponents of the federal ERA
could still make arguments about threats to the traditional understanding of women's roles in Virginia alongside arguments about the
possible impact on military service and abortion.

Alaska's ERA, passed in 1972, covered private and public conduct.
The state courts used the same standards for deciding ERA claims as
those utilized by the federal courts in Fourteenth Amendment sex
discrimination cases. This means that women in Alaska had more
protection against discrimination than women in Virginia, but less
than those in Illinois. Alaska had a number of antidiscrimination laws
on the books before the state ERA, but the state legislature made
substantial modifications in the state code to make it gender neutral.
The greatest gain for women in the state under the federal ERA would
be to require the use of a "strict scrutiny" standard, which would
require proof that a challenged law was based on a compelling state
interest to reach a necessary goal that could be reached in no other
way.[51]

In Colorado's 1972 state ERA, the courts had persistently used "clos-
est judicial scrutiny" for deciding claims, including the provision of
different treatment reasonably related and genuinely based on physical characteristics unique to one sex. This result accorded with the
practice in Illinois and followed closely the analysis in the legislative
history of the federal Equal Rights Amendment. The legislature also
undertook a general review of the statutes to make them gender neutral after the state ERA was enacted.[52]

Also in 1972, Hawaii added an equal rights amendment to its constitution. The state supreme court did not determine the proper standard for review, but upheld a rule requiring female, but not male,
visitors to an all-male prison to wear brassieres. A rule it found to
survive both the "substantially related" and "strict scrutiny" tests. In
every session since 1972 the state legislature acted to revise the code
and constitution to bring them into conformity with the state ERA.[53]

Connecticut's ERA, dating from 1974, covers private and public
conduct. At the time of the federal ratification effort, the supreme
court, like the one in Hawaii, left open the possibility that it would

use the "strict scrutiny" test. The state already had several antidiscrimination laws on the books before 1974, and because the legislature quickly changed numerous state laws to make them gender neutral, there was virtually no litigation in Connecticut.[54]

Maryland's ERA of 1972, like the one in Utah, also covers private conduct. The legislature and the courts were assiduous in enforcing an absolute standard even higher than "strict scrutiny" to make the ERA a viable tool for striking down discrimination. A challenged law had to be absolutely necessary to reach an essential state legislative goal. In 1977 in *Rand* v. *Rand,* the state's highest court asserted that sex could not be a factor in determining the parental child support obligation which had previously been attributed to fathers.[55]

Massachusetts's 1976 ERA, like those in Utah and Maryland, also covers private conduct. The state legislature enacted a series of bills to create gender neutrality in the law. Furthermore, state courts required a standard even more rigid than strict scrutiny, what seemed at times to be an absolute ban on sex-based classifications.[56]

The Montana 1972 ERA also applies to state and private actions. The legislature made substantial modifications in the state code to bring equality of treatment to women and men. However, the state's supreme court persisted in using the less rigid test elaborated by the U.S. Supreme Court in sex discrimination cases and had not used "strict scrutiny" as a standard.[57]

New Hampshire's 1974 ERA covers state action only. There had been only one case as of 1982, and in it the court did not decide the standard of review to be used. In this case, *Buckner* v. *Buckner,* the court decided that to permit alimony for a wife but not a husband violated the state ERA. The legislature partially reformed the state code, but several provisions remained, such as maximum hours provisions for women and the amount of night work they could do, different minimum ages for marriage for males and females, and sex-based language to define separate property and liability for spousal debts. Considering the inactivity in the state, it could have been argued during the ratification period that greater impact could be had under a federal ERA.[58]

New Mexico's ERA of 1973 which covers both private and state action on its face, was assumed by the state's attorney general to cover only state action. The courts did not articulate the standard of review to be used. The state attorney general asserted that, based on the history of the federal amendment, absolute prohibition or strict scrutiny must be the standard. After a systematic study undertaken upon the ratification of the state ERA, the legislature revised the state laws, changing twenty-six statutes and two constitutional amendments in the 1973 session. The state still, however, had a maximum hours of

work for women law and one which made it justifiable homicide for
a husband to kill someone in order to prevent an unlawful action
against his wife. No similar defense existed for wives who were defending their husbands.[59]

Pennsylvania's ERA of 1971 led to far-reaching changes in legislation and in court decisions in which an almost absolute standard of
review was used. The language of the amendment is substantially
similar to that of the proposed federal amendment except that it does
not have a state action requirement. It was used to require an equal
right of support for both sexes, to give married women and men the
right to use their own names, to equalize grounds for divorce for both
partners, to gender neutralize alimony, to allocate child support according to each parent's ability to pay, to recognize a wife's contribution as homemaker in distributing property upon divorce, and to
invalidate the minimum height requirement for police officers. In
addition, the Pennsylvania legislature undertook a massive review of
the statutes. Indeed, Pennsylvania had been making maximum use
of the ERA and had no reason not to ratify the federal amendment.[60]

Texas's 1972 ERA also covers private conduct, but the courts held
that it required governmental involvement. The courts held that sex
is a suspect classification that requires "strict scrutiny," but there was
no comprehensive review of state laws. However, some legislation was
passed including making spousal support and child support gender
neutral, granting that both parents can be natural guardians of their
minor children, and guaranteeing that credits and loans must be extended without regard to sex.[61]

Washington's 1972 ERA was interpreted as an absolute prohibition
against classification based on gender except where unique physical
characteristics permit differential treatment or affirmative action is
required. The state supreme court in 1975 said that by ratifying the
amendment citizens "intended to do more than what was already con-
tained in the otherwise governing constitutional provisions, Federal
and state, by which discrimination based on sex was permissible under
the rational relationship and strict scrutiny tests." Also, an omnibus
bill was passed in the legislature in 1973 to implement review of the
state's code to bring it into compliance with ERA.[62]

Wyoming's ERA dates from 1890, but there was an express provision preventing women from working in mines that was not repealed
until 1980. The language of the state provisions lent themselves to a
weaker standard than "strict scrutiny," although few cases had been
brought and the courts had not articulated a clear standard. There
was no general legislative review movement by 1982 and some sex-
based statutes remained unchallenged in the code, including seats and

rest periods for women workers only and no work for female children in many occupations during certain hours.[63]

Unlike the states without ERAs, in which such matters as the husband's responsibility for providing financial support for the family might still be controversial, the states with effective state ERAs had less cause for disputes over whether ERA should be ratified. Illinois, Washington, Texas, Pennsylvania, New Mexico, Maryland, Massachusetts, Connecticut, Hawaii, and Colorado had practically no reason; and Montana, New Hampshire, and Wyoming had little reason not to ratify ERA based on the existence of strong ERA implementation possibilities in their states. Virginia and Utah had every reason to oppose the federal ERA since their own ERAs had been enforced narrowly. In states with broad ERA enforcement, refusal to support a federal ERA had to be focused on issues beyond state control, such as the draft or federal funding for abortion. Some states that passed state ERAs contemporaneous with the federal ERA debated most of the same issues at the same time which indicates that within their borders a broad consensus existed not only for immediate approval of the federal ERA, but to take positive action within the state. In those states the federal action served to stimulate state responses. The states with no ERAs or narrow ERAs, or a pattern of nonimplementation when challenges were brought, would naturally not be favorably disposed toward a federal ERA that might necessitate substantial changes in traditional roles. The proponents should have expected Utah and Virginia not to ratify. The Illinois case was more surprising, but after the quick organization of the opponents, a difficult struggle could have been predicted.

The attempt to gain ratification of a federal ERA did affect the path of legal developments in the courts and in the states. Some state ERAs predate the 1972 passage of the federal amendment in Congress, and some have come after. But the existence or nonexistence of a state ERA without an analysis of its uses offered little guidance as to whether a federal amendment would be ratified by the state's legislature.

During the latter stages of the federal amendment ratification campaign, the Supreme Court continued to decide cases providing greater women's equality without reaching the "strict scrutiny" standard that a federal ERA could impose. But the more the Court tended toward expanding equality, the less force arguments for a federal amendment had. Indeed, the absence of a state ERA, or the nonenforcement of an existing one with a negative pattern of Supreme Court decisions, provided a better case for the approval of a federal ERA than legal developments tending toward greater equality. Patterns of enhanced legal protection made the case harder rather than easier to make. Proponents of ERA needed to hope for more negative decisions and state inaction, while opponents benefited from the persistence of a positive pattern. Vigorous implementation of state ERAs and court decisions tending toward more equality only helped to undermine any sense of urgency and to build consensus against ratification. On the other hand, negative implementation and court action could have helped engender a perception of necessity required to build consensus for ERA's approval.

Losing Consensus
in the Congress 9

By the time the extended deadline for ERA expired without ratification the proponents' failure to differentiate adequately between what was needed for state-by-state consensus and for national consensus had become obvious. In addition, proponents soon became aware that the eroding consensus for ERA affected their ability to gain support on other women's rights issues. A renewed attempt to gain passage of ERA in the House failed, and a number of other issues concerning women's rights were resolved or died for lack of support in the period before the 1984 elections.

In January 1983, when Speaker O'Neill, bent on showing the Democratic party's concern about the issue, reintroduced ERA into the Congress, the amendment's supporters were wary. During the intervening six months since the failure to gain ratification, they had become much more realistic about the amendment's prospects. Understanding the ratification process much better now, they knew success would be chancy at best. The same states that previously failed to ratify or attempted rescissions would most likely still oppose ratification. In those states not enough amendment supporters had been elected to state legislatures. NWPC chair Kathy Wilson and NOW president Judy Goldsmith, and other ERA proponents thought of asking that the amendment not be introduced or that its consideration be delayed or that the time for ratification be extended. But they decided that to ask for a delay or for a change in the time limit would be regarded as signs of weakness and might undermine grassroots mobilization for women's rights issues. So, they worked assiduously to ensure good testimony on the "irrelevant horribles" such as homosexuality and abortion. They expected the House to pass the amendment but worried about the Senate, where it was introduced on January 25, 1983. They felt confident that it would either not pass in the Republican controlled Senate or pass with crippling amendments that would make it unacceptable to the House.[1]

When the amendment came before the House Judiciary Subcommittee on Civil and Constitutional Rights, questions, especially from Republican members led by ranking Congressman James Sensenbrenner of Wisconsin, focused on crippling issues raised earlier in the state legislatures. The discussion centered on such concerns as abortion, whether persons could be sex segregated in prisons, whether women could be forced into combat, whether women's colleges would be denied federal funds or exemptions, and the effect of ERA on veterans' preference. The testimony in the Senate Judiciary Subcommittee on the Constitution took a similar direction after a series of pointed questions on those issues by Chairman Orrin Hatch (R, Utah) to Paul Tsongas (D, Mass.), the lead witness for the amendment. These congressional opponents were reiterating points anti-ERA leaders had made effectively in the ratification struggle as a continuing strategy. For example, Phyllis Schlafly still insisted that ERA would require the draft of eighteen-year-old girls, would require the payment of federal funds for abortion, and would mandate gay/lesbian rights. As Schlafly put it, "The burden of proof is on the ERA case to prove these things won't happen, and they cannot prove that. There is only one way to insure ERA won't do these things, and that is by including specific prohibitions in the text of ERA itself."[2]

It quickly became evident that the issues aired during the ratification debates had poisoned the congressional well. Not the principle of equality of rights but the argument for traditional male and female roles and family values would be the focus of the debate. Obtaining approval of an unamended ERA, a clean bill with the original language advanced since 1923, would be difficult indeed. After the hearings, it appeared that an amended ERA could be passed in the Senate before the November 18, 1983 adjournment, which would permit Republicans to argue they were for equal rights before the 1984 elections. Speaker O'Neill was determined to have the House go on record one way or the other on ERA before the end of the session. Leading supporters of the amendment in the Congressional Women's Caucus, such as Patricia Schroeder (D, Colo.) and Mary Rose Oakar (D, Ohio) agreed that it should be brought to a vote so long as an amended version did not pass. They pointed out that if an amended version passed the House and Senate, proponents would be in the uncomfortable position of having to oppose ratification in the states.[3]

The leadership of NOW and NWPC met with House leaders who decided to bring the amendment to the floor with a closed rule that would not permit amendments. Members would therefore have to vote a clean bill up or down. NOW and NWPC leaders believed the amendment might pass under those circumstances. Whether it did or not, they would be satisfied since they had decided not to oppose the amendment's introduction. If it passed, they could concentrate on the Senate, and if the Senate did not pass a clean bill, the amendment would fail because the House would not accept the amendments. The Republican opposition could then be a 1984 campaign issue. If the House also failed to pass the amendment, they would target members who voted against it in the 1984 congressional elections.[4]

Following this strategy, on November 15, 1983, Peter Rodino (D, N.J.), chairman of the House Judiciary Committee, introduced House Joint Resolution 1 on a motion to suspend the rules so that no floor amendments would be permitted. Although other amendments had been enacted under a similar procedure of suspension, most recently the Twenty-fourth or poll tax amendment, critics immediately jumped on the suspension as an unfair effort to cut off debate. The argument in the House took two tacks. Some argued that suspension was improper for such an important matter. Others argued against passage because it would change traditional rules regarding veterans' preference for male veterans, legalize homosexual marriages, legalize federal funding of abortions, legalize the use of women in combat, and upset marriage and family relations laws in the states.[5]

A number of members spoke before the introduction of the amendment, revising and extending their remarks to make their case. Sonny Montgomery (D, Miss.) pointed out that veterans' organizations opposed the amendment because "certain veteran preference laws would be challenged in the Federal courts." If the amendment would change the law on this subject, "Members should know that the twenty-eight million veterans who have answered our Nation's call in time of war would work hard in every state throughout the country to insure that the amendment is not ratified." Mrs. Marilyn Lloyd (D, Tenn.), Bill McCollum (R, Fla.), John Hammerschmidt (R, Ark.), and Christopher Smith (R, N.J.) all repeated the same point.[6]

Mrs. Lloyd and Mr. Howard Nielson (R, Utah) made the strongest extended arguments against ERA on all of the issues that had been advanced. Mrs. Lloyd supported an Equal Rights Amendment, but one "consistent with both equal rights for women and pro family issues." She wanted an amendment which would correct the discrimination women faced but not "rend the fabric of family life, or the institutions which this society has developed to protect a basic set of family values that are commensurate with family life." Amendments would "make explicit that nothing in the proposed amendment be construed to expand, endorse, or serve either the right to abortion, or the right to, or granting of Federal funds for the performance of abortion, except in those limited instances which the Congress has already defined." She wanted an explicit exclusion of homosexuals or homosexual marriages from the protections of the amendment. She also wanted a statement that tax exemptions could not be denied to sex-segregated schools because, "If the courts have to interpret sex discrimination in the same way that they interpret race discrimination then the Bob Jones University case [in which the Supreme Court said tax exemptions must be denied to schools that discriminate on the basis of race] makes very clear the potential risk to these institutions." She also wanted an explicit provision "that the amendment does not require the drafting of women into the armed forces of the United States, nor should it be construed as requiring women members of the armed forces to be assigned to combat duty." In addition, she wanted language making it clear that although most people who received veterans' preference are men and those who have abortions are women, outlawing abortion and ending veterans' preference would not be required by ERA.[7]

Mrs. Lloyd also wanted to have language which would prevent construing the amendment to "deprive wives or widows of rights or benefits granted to them by the states, or to interfere with state laws that obligate husbands to support their wives." An amendment should also make clear that distinctions between the sexes to protect personal modesty would be permitted. "This stipulation would protect such institutions as private schools, hospitals, prisons and other public accommodations from being put in the position of having to implement sex-integration policies. . . ." She particularly objected to Section 2 of the amendment which denied states the opportunity to draw distinctions between men and women if they chose to do so. She thought this was "both unwarranted and less effective than reliance on the states."[8]

Nielson of Utah repeated many of these same points during the debate adding that "special protection laws which women's unions have worked for years to achieve would be thrown out in one fell swoop." Furthermore the insurance industry could not distinguish between women and men which would mean that "women, who have better and safer driving records, and live healthier and longer lives would lose the advantage they now enjoy in insurance." When Utah considered ERA he was Speaker of the House. After Utah voted negatively he had this to say: "Many who had previously given little thought to the implications of the amendment began to study it more carefully to determine just what effect ERA would have on our society." Now it had become clear, he said, that "the type of society that this misguided amendment would create is against the interests and desires of the American people." He would, however, support ERA if it had amendments to keep it from applying "to abortion and abortion funding, personal privacy, military service for women, et cetera."[9]

The proponents of ERA argued that it was a long overdue amendment desired by the American people and necessary if women were to achieve legal equality. They pointed out its irrelevancy to the family issues that had been raised. As Schroeder (D, Colo.) asserted, members say, " 'Well, we ought to put in everything it does not mean.' Well, if we put in everything it does not mean, it would be 800 pages long. We have never put in the Constitution what it does not mean. We did not do it under the freedom of speech, under the freedom of religion, or any other amendment to the Constitution." Barbara Mikulski (D, Md.) explained how the state ERAs in Pennsylvania and Maryland had been important tools for recognizing the economic contributions of homemakers and improving women's economic life. They had not destroyed the family but helped it.[10]

Geraldine Ferraro (D, N.Y.) explained how ERA would help to strike overtly discriminatory laws from state and federal statute books and would require reform of other supposedly sex neutral laws that discriminated against women. Oakar and Schroeder emphasized that ERA would really be an economic rights amendment. Oakar, an opponent of legal abortion, emphasized that economic justice for all "is an extension of pro-life philosophy." Pro-lifers, who opposed abortion, needed, she said, to be concerned about "the quality of life of working women and homemakers who are discriminated against in the work field and are discriminated against in the insurance area." Furthermore, "In several states with ERA's, the state ERA was argued to the courts as a ground for overturning restrictions on state funding for abortion. In not one of these cases was a state ERA used by the court in its decisions to overturn the restrictions."[11]

Some who grounded their opposition on the suspension of the rules procedure argued, as did Hamilton Fish (R, N.Y.), that "the procedure will not permit the 404 members who are not members of the House Judiciary Committee to consider the merits of amendments many of us thought reflected legitimate concerns." Fish also asserted that although he was a cosponsor, he objected to a procedure that denied consideration of "amendments which we might even pass." Some noted that a *Washington Post* editorial that morning had commented negatively on the procedure. Edwards of Oklahoma asserted Democrats had "made a serious political blunder and you will not laugh last." Carlos Moorhead (R, Calif.) opposed the procedure while introducing a detailed legal memorandum he had been given by a law firm explaining how the amendment could affect insurance classifications. If the intent was to affect insurance, the memorandum explained that it would "not prohibit gender based classifications."[12]

Newt Gingrich (R, Ga.) opposed the procedures by asserting the need for amendments if ERA had any possibility of gaining ratification. Thomas DeWine (R, Ohio), a member of the Judiciary Com-

mittee, opposed the closed rule also and insisted an open rule was
needed to "get the amendments, get it cleaned up and let us go pass
it." Clay Shaw (R, Fla.) wanted amendments also. To those who opposed amendments, he asserted, "ERA was not carved in stone by
God." Its imperfections needed to be changed, such as the issue of
using women in combat. Marge Roukema (R, N.J.) supported the ERA
but worried about whether the expedited procedure would be "another impediment to an already controversial proposal" in the ratification process.[13]

The worries proponents had when ERA was introduced were justified. When the votes were taken on November 14, 1983, the amendment failed to gain the needed two-thirds of the House. There were
278 yeas and 147 nays, six votes short of the required majority. The
Democrats divided 225–38 in favor and the Republicans opposed it
109–53.[14] The table below shows the breakdown by state.[15]

Some members truly objected to what Hamilton Fish called the
"cavalier fashion" in which the amendment was proposed. However,
Speaker O'Neill was probably right when he asserted, "In your hearts,

ERA Vote, November 14, 1983

	No	Total		No	Total
Alabama	4	6	Nevada	2	2
Arkansas	2	4	New Jersey	2	10
Arizona	3	5	New Mexico	1	3
California	12	40	New York	7	29
Colorado	2	6	N. Carolina	3	8
Florida	9	19	Ohio	9	16
Georgia	5	8	Oklahoma	1	3
Idaho	2	2	Oregon	2	5
Illinois	9	18	Pennsylvania	8	19
Indiana	5	8	Rhode Island	1	2
Iowa	2	4	S. Carolina	3	5
Kansas	3	4	Tennessee	6	7
Kentucky	4	4	Texas	10	24
Louisiana	3	6	Utah	3	3
Michigan	4	16	Virginia	5	10
Minnesota	2	8	W. Virginia	1	2
Mississippi	3	4	Wisconsin	2	6
Missouri	5	6	Wyoming	1	1
Montana	1	1			

Total "No" Votes 147

you know those of you who have taken this floor, that there is no way this amendment would pass under an open rule with either one of those amendments [abortion exclusion and draft exclusion]." He explained that he had taken the burden of scheduling the bill himself to try to get a "lean, clean bill that suits the amendment of the Constitution." If members wanted, he said, "to hide behind something that we have done, the structure in which we have brought it up, you are not fooling anybody. In your heart you will never live it down. You are looking for an escape."[15]

If the votes of the congressmen are any guide to what would have happened in the ratification process, Georgia, Arkansas, Indiana, Montana, South Carolina, Virginia, and Rhode Island would have been doubtful as supporters of an unamended ERA. Seven states— Alabama, Arizona, Kansas, Kentucky, Mississippi, Missouri, and Tennessee—had majorities against ERA. The entire delegations from Idaho, Nevada, Utah, and Wyoming voted negatively. In the previous campaign for ERA, Tennessee, Kentucky, and Idaho had, along with South Dakota and Nebraska, rescinded their ratifications; and Georgia, South Carolina, Arizona, Alabama, Mississippi, Missouri, Nevada, and Utah had never ratified in the first place. Wyoming, by a 40–21 vote in the House and a 17–12 Senate vote, had ratified in 1973. Indiana, by a 54–45 House and a 26–24 Senate vote, ratified in 1977. Kansas had ratified in 1972 by an 86–37 House and a 34–58 Senate vote. Montana ratified in 1974 by a 73–23 House and a 28–22 Senate vote. Rhode Island ratified in 1972 by a 70–12 House and a 39–11 Senate vote. What the 1983 vote represented was confused somewhat by the insertion of the suspension of the rules issue, but at best it reflected an erosion of support in some states and continued recalcitrance in others, while Nebraska and South Dakota members voted for it despite earlier rescissions in their states. Given the fact that only thirteen states were needed to deny ratification, Congressional passage again could have been premature.[17]

In response to the House action, proponents issued the expected public denunciations. Kathy Wilson of the National Women's Political Caucus said, "We've seen the truth of where legislators stand and I hope they'll see the consequences." Judy Goldsmith of the National Organization for Women said, "Today's vote shows that Republicans understand neither the determination women have to finally win passage of the ERA, nor the political realities of the gender gap in 1984." Privately, however, ERA leaders were relieved. They conceded that the failure bought them more time to organize on the issues, to gain more pro-ERA state legislators, and to decide whether to assault frontally the issues such as veterans' preference, abortion, and combat duty for women or to continue to attempt to ignore them.[18]

An underlying aspect of the committee hearings and the debate on
the floor was a deep distrust of the role of federal courts in the American system of government, which opponents of strong federal action
since the 1930s had gradually inculcated as part of their political ideology. Opponents of ERA kept insisting that proponents had to make
sure the courts could never interpret the amendment to reach any
result they might find objectionable. Some members who argued in
this fashion did so because they knew courts use legislative history to
interpret the law, including Constitutional amendments. They wanted
to be sure that legislative history ruled out pro-abortion funding, anti-
veterans' preference decisions, and combat duty for women. Other
members seemed to be attacking the traditional role of the federal
judiciary in interpreting the law, insisting that at least in the case of
ERA, the courts should have their hands tied. Such an attitude, if
broadly adopted, would undermine some fundamental concepts of
the American constitutional system: (1) that the Constitution is not
like a statute book containing detailed specifics to govern every im-
aginable situation, but instead is written in broad terms in order to
be flexible and last for the ages even when unforseen circumstances
arise; and (2) that the courts are the final arbiter, of state-federal
disputes in order to maintain the roles appropriate to a federal system
of government. Indeed, these aspects of the debate may not have been
thought out in such terms. However, many of the congressmen who
argued in this fashion had supported various measures to strip the
federal courts of the power to rule in controversial cases involving
school desegregation, affirmative action, abortion, and other hotly
contested issues. The problem for ERA proponents before 1983
seemed to be gaining enough states in which consensus existed. After
the congressional vote, they needed also to re-establish a national
consensus. Congressmen seemed more inclined than ever to vote their
constituents' fears rather than their hopes.[19]

In the spring of 1984, women reformers in Congress, still persuaded
that despite the ERA vote the much-talked-about gender gap would
make their colleagues more receptive to women's concerns before the
1984 elections, pressed for one part of the Economic Equity Act, a
proposal to end sex discrimination in insurance. These women still
did not understand that the fate of this provision, as well as other
pieces of the Act, was jeopardized from the beginning by the failure
to adopt the principle of equality embodied in the ERA. They expressed dismay when the insurance measure was gutted by a House
committee on March 28, 1984, after the insurance industry mounted
a fierce lobbying campaign against it. A compromise worked out by
Congressman James Florio (D, N.J.) and Barbara Milkuski (D, Md.),

which answered most of the industry's arguments, did not carry the day. Congressmen Wayne Dowdy (D, Miss.), Norman Lent (R, N.Y.) and Billy Tauzin (D, La.) offered amendments which were adopted by the committee by a 23–18 vote, stripping the legislation of its force. Proponents planned to reintroduce the legislation in 1985, but the gender gap obviously did not prove a forceful enough basis for passage. In the interim, the NOW Legal Defense and Education Fund embarked on a series of discrimination suits, under state laws, against insurance companies, beginning with a class action suit against Mutual of Omaha in the District of Columbia.[20]

But some pieces of the Economic Equity Act which recognized women's traditional roles found favor with the Congress. A bill introduced in the House of Representatives by Congresswoman Barbara Kennelly (D, Conn.) in November 1983 to set up a strong system of child support enforcement finally passed. Kennelly, the only woman member of the House Ways and Means Committee, cited data showing that 8.2 million women were single heads of households with at least one child living at home in 1982, only 59 percent were awarded any child support, and fewer than half received full payment. She noted that almost $4 billion in court-ordered child support went unpaid in 1982, and that the 1975 child support federal law gave matching funds to states to collect support from spouses on welfare but other mothers received no help. The Kennelly bill passed the House and the Senate where it was introduced by Senator David Durenberger (R, Minn.) and Senator Bill Bradley (D, N.J.). The bills directed states to set up systems for withholding support from wages after it has been 30 days overdue and included all spouses, not just those on welfare. It was supported by Secretary of Health and Human Services Margaret Heckler and signed into law by the president on August 18, 1984.[21]

The bill to reform private pension plans, the Retirement Equity Act of 1983, was sponsored originally by Congresswoman Geraldine Ferraro (D, N.Y.). In 1982 only 10.3 percent of women over age sixty-five received an average pension of $2,585, and only five to ten percent of surviving spouses received pension benefits. The bill, shepherded through the House by Kennelly and through the Senate by Senator Robert Dole (R, Kan.), head of the Senate Finance Committee, lowered the age for vesting, required automatic survivors benefits in private plans unless both spouses waived them, and liberalized break-in-service rules to take into account women's more frequent departures from the workforce. It also clarified the authority of state courts to distribute pension benefits in divorce, a significant acknowledgment of the work done by homemakers in a marriage. The president signed the bill on August 23, 1984.[22]

The issues of pension reform and child support enforcement did not challenge women's traditional roles and in fact were reinforcing. Each encouraged women to play traditional maternal and housewife roles while making provisions for the sometimes traumatic economic consequences that ensued. Another piece of legislation introduced by Congresswoman Mary Rose Oakar (D, Ohio) had less benign tendencies and met failure. In January 1984, Oakar introduced her federal employees pay equity legislation by proposing modifications and study of the federal position classification system to evaluate whether it led to discriminatory wage-setting practices and discriminatory wage differentials within the federal government. The Office of Personnel Management would conduct the study. After the legislation passed in the House, the Senate refused to meet in conference on the bill because of the addition of the pay equity study as an amendment to merit pay and Senior Executive Service provisions. The bill was passed without the pay equity study, but with a provision requiring the General Accounting Office to do an initial analysis of the scope of a more complete examination of federal pay practices. Although its chances appeared slim, Congresswoman Oakar reintroduced a similar bill when the Ninety-eighth Congress convened in early 1985. Essentially, what happened to the Economic Equity Act by the end of 1984 was only an example of the hard times the women's rights movement had fallen on, despite all of the talk about women's increasing political importance. Proposals to give tax credits to companies that hired displaced homemakers and to increase tax deductions for child care expenses also failed of passage in the Congress on the grounds that they were too expensive.[23]

In the meanwhile, comparable worth, or pay equity, continued to be a major issue for women seeking to end what they regarded as wage bias. In the states, lawsuits to enforce pay equity were in process by 1985 in California, Illinois, and Missouri. New Jersey enacted a pay equity study bill on October 27, 1984, and striking clerical workers at Yale University won a contract on January 23, 1985, which the workers characterized as containing pay equity elements. In Minnesota, state officials began, in January 1983, to implement a four-year, $2.2 million effort to balance sex-based disparities in pay in state employment.

In the meantime, the state of Washington appealed a December 1983 ruling by U.S. District Court Judge Jack Tanner to the Ninth Circuit, that the state had intentionally discriminated against 15,000 employees in female-dominated categories by paying them less than males in jobs requiring equivalent skills, effort and responsibility, despite a job evaluation study documenting the disparity. On November

26, 1984, the U.S. Supreme Court declined to decide the issue of comparable worth by refusing review to a U.S. Ninth Circuit ruling against women nursing faculty of the University of Washington. The women claimed that the university violated Title VII of the Civil Rights Act of 1964 by paying the mostly female, nursing professors lower average salaries than the faculty of other departments. The Title VII claim was rejected, the lower court said, because the nurses at trial failed to prove either disparate treatment or disparate impact required by the Supreme Court 1971 *Griggs* v. *Duke Power* decision. Disparate impact refers to employer practices that are fair in form but discriminatory in operation. Disparate treatment requires the plaintiff to prove by a preponderance of the evidence that the imbalance is the result of a discriminatory animus or intent. The nurses case, in bypassing the issue of comparable worth, left open the possibility that the Supreme Court would ultimately decide the issue in the AFSCME (American Federation of State, County, and Municipal Employees) case appeal.[24]

The Reagan administration in addition to opposing Congresswoman Oakar's pay equity proposal, indicated its opposition in other ways. William Niskanen, member of the White House Council of Economic Advisors denounced the concept as a "truly crazy proposal" during the 1984 presidential campaign. Clarence M. Pendleton, Jr., Reagan-appointed chairman of the U.S. Civil Rights Commission, denounced it after the election at a November press conference as the "looniest idea since Looney Tunes came on the screen." The chairman's comment, which came in advance of any commission report or fact-finding on the issue, and Pendleton's and Niskanen's views were characteristic of criticisms of the concept. While women pointed to evidence of a persistent pay gap between women and men, opponents attributed any gap to women choosing, because of the family roles they play or expect to play, certain jobs which happen to fit in with their schedules, even when they pay less. Any serious attempt to implement pay equity would of course require financing to raise women's salaries but would challenge the idea that men should play certain roles and hold certain jobs while women should play different roles. When asked, for example, whether he felt married male breadwinners are entitled to higher wages than either single men or women, Pendleton replied, "You have to give some kind of respect to traditional family values." As June O'Neill of the Urban Institute described the arguments against comparable worth: "Both the occupational differences and the pay gap to a large extent are the result of differences in the roles of women and men in the family and the effects these role differences have on the accumulation of skills and other job choices that affect pay." Black women, who have disproportionately always had to work, were mostly ignored as factors in the discussion. For them at least, arguments about whether the issue had arisen because women have only recently become breadwinners bore a ring of unreality.[25]

While the discussion of pay equity or comparable worth proceeded, the U.S. Commissioner of Labor Statistics, Janet L. Norwood, pointed out that the majority of working women are in both low-paying jobs and industries. Furthermore, the decline of manufacturing in the United States has blocked women's entrance into higher paying, blue collar jobs in the automobile, steel, and rubber industries. Since 1960, women's wages have remained at approximately 57 to 65 percent of those of men. A Rand Corporation study predicted that by the year 2000 women would be paid at roughly 74 percent of the level attained by men. This fact was acknowledged as having great impact on efforts to stem the increasing femininization of poverty and its effect on women and children in female-headed households. Whatever the outcome of litigation on the issue, proponents will have great difficulty gaining general acceptance for pay equity. The difficulty stems, as it did for the proponents of ERA, largely from the persistence of assumptions about the roles and functions of women and men, no matter what roles they play in society.[26]

In addition to the comparable worth cases and the Supreme Court decision in *Grove City* v. *Bell* weakening the enforcement possibilities of Title IX of the Education Amendments of 1972, the Court has recently decided a number of other important cases that shed light on the prospects for women's rights and the Equal Rights Amendment. In *Hishon* v. *King*, the Supreme Court decided that the provisions of Title VII apply to law firm decisions to name partners. Hishon's sex discrimination claim did not present novel or difficult issues, since it involved an individual claim and not the more controversial issues of the scope of affirmative action in cases involving groups. The decision can be regarded as a victory for women's rights, in that Hishon won, but gives little guidance on how the Court might regard issues of more wide-ranging significance.[27]

In state of *Arizona* v. *Norris* on July 5, 1983, the Supreme Court ruled that an employer violated Title VII of the Civil Rights Act of 1964 by offering its employees retirement options which resulted in paying a woman lower benefits than a man who had made the same contribution. But the decision applied only to contributions collected after August 1, 1983, thus denying retroactive relief. In October 1984, the Court allowed a limited retroactive application of the *Norris* decision. Without comment, the justices let stand a ruling that would reduce the pension checks of some male college faculty members to equalize them with the monthly retirement pay received by their female colleagues. The Court let stand a Second Circuit Court of Appeals decision involving Teachers Insurance and Annuity Association and the College Retirement Equities Fund that covered approximately 700,000 employees at 3,400 colleges and universities, which extended the date to fund contributions even when made prior to August 1, 1983. The Second Circuit had agreed with an EEOC ruling that "the reduction in benefits to males is not inequitable in the absence of any settled expectation of the males concerning the level of their future benefits."[28]

In July 1984, the Supreme Court decided that the United States Jaycees violated the Minnesota Human Rights Act by excluding women from membership. The Court, in reversing the Eighth Circuit Court of Appeals, decided that accepting women as regular members did not abridge male members' freedom of association, in that non-members frequently participated in many of the central activities of the organization. Also, Minnesota's compelling interest in eradicating discrimination against female citizens justified any impact the Act's enforcement might have on the male members' freedom of association. Nothing in the record indicated that admission of women as members would interfere with the Jaycees' ability to engage in its constitutionally protected civic, charitable, lobbying, fundraising, and other activities or to disseminate its preferred views. Justice Brennan in his majority opinion for which four joined, acknowledged that Minnesota's law reached various forms of public, quasi-commercial conduct.

> This expansive definition reflects a recognition of the changing nature of the American economy and of the importance both to the individual and society of removing the barriers to economic advancement and political and social integration that have historically plagued certain disadvantaged groups including women.

Justice O'Connor concurred in the judgment but wrote her own opinion in which she indicated she would have voted differently if the Jaycees were an entirely expressive association without involvement in commercial activities. If the activity is predominantly of the type protected under the First Amendment then she would permit sex discrimination. She cited the Girl and Boy Scouts in her opinion. The Jaycees, she agreed, were engaged in "the art of solicitation and management." She agreed the state had a "legitimate interest in ensuring nondiscriminatory access to the commercial opportunity presented by membership in the Jaycees."[29]

On June 12, 1984, in *Firefighters Union* v. *Stotts*, the Supreme Court

ruled that white males with seniority could not be laid off first in order
to retain blacks who had been hired only after an affirmative action
plan overturned an employer's policy of not hiring blacks on the basis
of race. Even though the Supreme Court did not decide the issue,
the administration announced that the decision sounded the death
knell for all gender-conscious or race-conscious remedies such as
goals, timetables, or quotas even after discrimination had been proven.
Such provisions had been widely used and approved by the Supreme
Court, were not at issue in the *Stotts* case, and continued to gain federal
court approval even after *Stotts* was decided. But the Justice Department continued to pursue a policy of active opposition to such remedies whether voluntary or not, which influenced efforts to open
employment opportunities to women of all races and minorities from
which they had been previously excluded on the ground of race or
gender.[30]

In addition to the Supreme Court decisions, in late September 1984,
the Commonwealth Court of Pennsylvania upheld state laws restrict-
ing the use of Medicaid funds for abortions. The court reversed a
lower court that found such laws violated both the equal protection
clause and the Equal Rights Amendment of the state constitution.
However, the Pennsylvania Supreme Court outlawed automobile insurance rates based on sex, as a violation of the state's insurance statutes and Equal Rights Amendment. Hawaii in 1974, North Carolina
in 1977, Massachusetts in 1978, and Michigan in 1981 had already
outlawed sex-based automobile insurance pricing. State Farm Insurance's lawyers in the Pennsylvania case asserted that the state court's
decision would hurt women who would pay higher rates as a result.
But women's groups said that if the industry used relevant variables
such as miles driven, previous accidents, and the like, instead of sex,
the rates would probably be lower and in any case fairer. So far no
state has outlawed sex-based rates in every form of insurance. James
J. McCabe, a Philadelphia lawyer representing State Farm, explained
that he concluded that under the reasoning of the Pennsylvania automobile insurance decision, sex-based rates in life or casualty insurance would probably also be found illegal under the state Equal Rights
Amendment. Most often insurance companies charged women higher
medical insurance rates on the basis of gender.[31]

As the 1984 elections approached, those female reformers who opposed the Reagan administration pointed to examples of how women's
rights had been retarded despite the gender gap. They noted that
the president and his appointees had weakened programs to fight job
and education discrimination. They pointed out how the administration had sided against equal educational opportunities for women,
despite pleas from women's organizations, including leading Repub-

licans in the February 1984 Supreme Court, *Grove City* case. They asserted that budget cuts had hit poor families the hardest, of which a disproportionate number were headed by women. Under Social Security, they noted, minimum benefits were cut for future recipients, 85 percent of whom were female. Furthermore, they emphasized that federal appointments of women (despite Sandra Day O'Connor's role as Supreme Court Justice) had lagged until the election came near. Even ardent women's rights activists in the president's own party, Jill Ruckelshaus and Mary Louise Smith, were dumped from the U.S. Commission on Civil Rights for criticizing the president's policies. These events led many Republican women's rights proponents to lean toward supporting the Democrats in the presidential campaign.[32]

During the 1981 electoral campaigns, women's groups and individuals who supported ERA and other women's issues received a very warm reception at the Democratic Platform Committee and at the Democratic Convention. On the other hand, opponents of such issues were embraced during the Republican electoral proceedings. The Democrats endorsed ratification of the unamended ERA and the remaining proposals in the Economic Equity Act, as well as comparable worth, and nominated Geraldine Ferraro for vice-president. At the National Women's Political Caucus convention in July 1983, where the Democratic candidates for the presidential nomination spoke, Jesse Jackson included a commitment to select a woman running mate as part of his campaign. In subsequent private meetings with Kathy Wilson, NWPC chair, and Judy Goldsmith, NOW president, he repeated that pledge in an effort to garner their support. In February 1984, NWPC started developing a coalition of NOW, NWPC, the Women's Campaign Fund, and other groups to advance the idea. They lobbied male public officials to give support to the idea. Many of them, including Speaker of the House of Representatives, Thomas P. O'Neill, endorsed the idea publicly.[33]

In June 1984, Kathy Wilson and Mondale aide, John Reilly met to discuss a female vice-presidential candidacy. They left Reilly a memo outlining the case for picking a woman—it would buttress the Mondale candidacy and they thought it was right. It was based primarily on the strength of the gender gap as a force to defeat President Reagan. NWPC also polled delegates to the convention and announced results showing that 74 percent believed a woman would help on the ticket. After NOW endorsed Mondale at their summer convention, they also promised support for Geraldine Ferraro as his running mate. NWPC instituted an elaborate whip system to use on the floor of the convention in July to ensure support for a woman vice-presidential nominee. After interviewing a number of candidates, Mondale met with a group of women political leaders who pressed him to choose a woman. When he did so, the women's groups were joyous and for the first time in its history, NWPC endorsed a ticket, the Mondale-Ferraro one, for the election in November.[34]

In their press to obtain the nomination of Ferraro and to ensure that it would actually come to pass once Mondale had agreed, the women's groups temporarily abandoned the political alliances they had made with black women. NOW endorsed several planks that Jesse Jackson proposed for inclusion in the Democratic platform at their summer convention, but withdrew their support at the Democratic Convention after Mondale had selected Ferraro. NWPC dismantled its whip system, which black women had thought they could utilize to gain support on a number of platform issues. These steps taken by the women's groups alienated large numbers of black women who were already angered by their failure to insist that Mondale interview any black women (including Shirley Chisholm), whether they were supporters of Gary Hart, Jesse Jackson, or Walter Mondale, during the widely publicized interviews for a vice-presidential candidate.[35]

At the Republican Platform Subcommittee in August, NWPC chair, Republican Mary Stanley, along with former Republican National Committee chair, Mary Louise Smith, and Maine Congresswoman J. Olympia Snowe, testified in favor of including ERA, the Women's Equity Act, the Civil Rights Act of 1984 and other measures in the platform. Despite their pleas, the party rejected these measures as well as unconditional rejection of the concept of pay equity or comparable worth. Afterwards Stanley noted, "I have been a Republican for all of my political life. I am proud to be a Republican and I am proud to be a feminist. These days, unfortunately, I sometimes have a difficult time being both."[36]

The harsh reception the women reformers received accelerated NOW and NWPC efforts to achieve the election of the Mondale-Ferraro ticket. But in the wake of disclosures about the financial affairs of Geraldine Ferraro and her husband, the euphoria of the Democratic Convention quickly dissipated. The breach in the alliance of black and white women occasioned by the proceedings at the convention did not heal entirely throughout the campaign. In August 1984, disaffected black women organized the National Political Congress of Black Women, chaired by Shirley Chisholm, to mobilize separately from the other major women's rights groups.[37]

When Ronald Reagan won reelection, the results showed a gender gap persisted, but smaller than that in 1980. Despite favorable public opinion polls and bipartisan support from the state's leadership, Maine's ERA went down to defeat by about the same margin as the Mondale-Ferraro ticket. In the blame-casting after what was a clear defeat for the women's movement, women's groups refused to take responsibility for the Mondale-Ferraro defeat. Dotty Lynch, a pollster who had originally been in the Hart campaign but worked with Mondale's staff in the general election, said women were asked to get out the vote "but we were never given the resources with which to achieve that." She continued, the Mondale people "blew a really grand opportunity" by not emphasizing the "sense of empowerment" the Ferraro victory could bring to women. Kathy Wilson of the NWPC said about Geraldine Ferraro, "There was some frustration among women's leaders that she talked deficits more than empowerment." Ann P. Lewis, political director of the Democratic National Committee, did not believe the women's movement had been eclipsed by the failure. "Our next set of desires will be made in an atmosphere of realism, and that's probably good for all of us," she said. "We didn't invent defeat. White men have been losing elections for years."[38]

Privately, women's groups leaders talked of the Ferraro candidacy as a good idea, but admitted they could never overcome the pall cast by the allegations over her finances. On the positive side, they pointed to the 934 women elected to state legislatures in 1984, which increased the numbers of women in legislatures from 991 in 1983, to 1067 after the 1984 elections. They emphasized an increase of one in women state treasurers, making a total of 11, and Republican Arlene Violet of Rhode Island elected as the first woman state attorney general. They also pointed to the twelve point gender gap in Vermont that helped to carry Madeline Kunin to victory in the governor's race. In addition, they stressed the important role women played in helping Paul Simon of Illinois, Tom Harkin in Iowa, and John Kerry in Massachusetts gain election to the Senate.[39]

Pollsters analyzing the election results in early 1985 reached several significant conclusions concerning women's participation in the presidential election. Female interest in politics did increase. Turnout increased by 2 percent over 1980 and 1976, to 61 percent of eligible voters. But the Republicans seemed to understand women's voting behavior better than did the Democrats. They broke women into categories based on age, whether they were working outside the home or not, or whether they were married or single. Then they focused on the primary concerns of each group, and targeted special advertising campaigns to each. The Mondale campaign, on the other hand, did little research on the women's vote and did no targeting of advertising at groups of women or women as a whole. Even Ferraro appeared in only one advertisement at the end of the campaign. Essentially the Mondale campaign did what proponents of ERA had done: they failed to understand that different groups of women have to be appealed to differently.[40]

Whatever points women's rights proponents made about the election in overall terms, the results reinforced the notion that large numbers of women did not vote on the basis of what would enhance women's equality. The women's movement prepared to keep reintroducing ERA on principle, but with the understanding that it would not actively be pursued in the Congress. They pledged to attempt passage of other women's rights legislation. But increasingly the public was treated to questions about the dangers to white men of women taking over non-traditional jobs, for example, in skilled trades and the construction industry. In 1984, 64.9 percent of the male population was employed, as compared to 70.2 percent at the beginning of the decade. In addition, discussion of the decline of the industrial sector and the increase of service industries in which women predominate, and increasing women in the professions, displacing men, permeated the environment. These discussions included ominous warnings about white men joining the underclass, and increasing divorce rates. One observer opined that, "At this point, it seems clear that the greatest adjustments will have to be made by men. But women will also have to face the prospect of living with men they have outpaced."[41]

When the Ninety-ninth Congress convened in January 1985, women's rights advocates began a new push for legislative proposals despite the election year set-backs. The Equal Rights Amendment was reintroduced again on January 3, the first day of the legislative season. Peter Rodino (D, N.J.), Patricia Schroeder (D, Colo.), Don Edwards (D, Calif.), and Hamilton Fish (R, N.Y.) sponsored ERA in the House as House Joint Resolution 2. In the Senate, Edward Kennedy (D, Mass.) introduced it as Senate Joint Resolution 10. The women's groups had an understanding with the cosponsors that the amendment would not be brought forward for votes. They did not want it passed, knowing that not enough votes existed for ratification and not even being sure, after the 1983 House results, that it would pass in that body. Elizabeth L. Chittick, president of the National Woman's party, opined that economic stress and the election results which showed "that the majority of people are leaning to the extreme right" meant a change in strategy to achieve ERA. She thought they must "change the name, 'women's issues' and broaden our base and call such issues 'economic issues affecting everyone'." But she said, "We will not give up on ERA until it becomes the law of the land."[42]

The strategy of trying to define women's rights issues in terms emphasizing their economic impact as a matter of egalitarian philosophy was followed by proponents as legislation was pursued in the Congress. The major effort for women's groups was focused on the Civil Rights Restoration Act of 1985 designed to overturn the February 1984 Supreme Court decision narrowing protection against sex discrimination in education programs. A legislative attempt in the Civil Rights Act of 1984 failed in the Senate, after passage by a 373–32 vote in the House in December 1984. The 1985 bill, like the 1984 measure, would apply to similar statutes prohibiting discrimination on the basis of race, solely because of handicapping condition, and age. The effort to pass the 1985 act, along with continued confrontations with the reconstituted U.S. Commission on Civil Rights and with the administration over employment discrimination issues, provided occasion for black and white women activists to work together, helping to heal the breach generated during the Democratic Convention and the subsequent presidential campaign.[43]

The Congressional Women's Caucus prepared a new Economic Equity Act building on the partial measures of 1984, in an effort to expand pension coverage further for women, to increase options for child care and to revise Social Security benefits to aid women. They hoped to gain support by emphasizing that these measures affected entire families. "When we talk about the need for child care, the need for pregnancy leave, these are not only feminist issues. These are human rights and family issues," according to Barbara Boxer (D, Calif.). She pointed out, "You can't keep the family together if one spouse is underpaid or can't get child care."[44] They recognized the negative political impact of the Mondale-Ferraro defeat, but hoped to emphasize the importance of women's votes in key congressional races to gain support in the Congress. Whether this emphasis would work or not would depend on how congressmen assessed the concerns of the different groups of women who had voted for them.

In the summer of 1985, as they continued lobbying for legislation in the Congress, the two major women's rights organizations elected new leadership to carry on the struggle. The National Women's Political Caucus elected Irene Natividad to succeed Kathy Wilson as chair. Thirty-six-year-old Natividad, a New York education administrator and the first Asian-American chair of the Caucus, had experience as a political insider as a vice-chair of the National Women's Political Caucus in the Democratic National Committee, and as Asian-American liaison in Geraldine Ferraro's campaign for vice-president. She described her goals as broadening the membership because, "like the rest of the women's movement our profile is white, age 30 and older, middle- or upper-class and highly educated." In addition to the NWPC's major work of trying to put women in political office, she would lobby for abortion rights and pay equity, and acknowledged the continued need for an ERA. Natividad's plans were predictable and seemed to keep the NWPC on the path of a low key approach to ERA while electing more proponents to state legislatures.[45]

But when former NOW president, Eleanor Smeal, defeated Judy

Goldsmith to lead the organization, an entirely different approach was approved. Smeal vowed to take women "back into the streets" over the issues, adopting a more direct action confrontational approach. She would emphasize abortion rights, the Civil Rights Restoration Act to overturn the *Grove City* decision, and passage of ERA. She would "take the ERA out of the deep freeze," proposing to spend $250,000 to support passage of a referendum for a state ERA that was on the ballot in Vermont in 1986. She thought pushing ERA would be "a wonderful organizing tool and consciousness-raiser." Also, even if ERA were not approved, "The ERA has always been our biggest money raiser."[46]

Whatever new or old departures are undertaken by the newly elected leaders of NOW and NWPC, what supporters of ERA need more than anything else, if they ever want to gain the ratification of the amendment, is a strategy based on an awareness of how successful amendment-making proceeded in the past. They must remember the importance of timing. Successful amendment-making on controversial issues took place during periods of reform and not during periods of reaction. They should take into account the importance of creating consensus state by state before an amendment receives congressional approval. ERA supporters need an effective public relations approach which can build a sense of necessity that the Constitution be perfected by including the principle of equality of rights for women as an essential component of republican government in a democratic society. They must persuade women in enough states that equality of rights is a principle they can embrace without doing harm to their lives and the lives of other females and males. Engendering a sense of necessity which would create consensus state by state in electing pro-ERA legislators, and at the same time maintaining enough national visibility and focus to build membership and attract funds needed to finance the strategy will not be easy. Until a program balancing these requirements exists, there will be no ERA in the Constitution.

Appendix: Selected Amendments and Proposed Amendments to the United States Constitution

ARTICLE V.
MODE OF AMENDMENT

The Congress, whenever two thirds of both Houses shall deem it necessary, shall propose Amendments to this Constitution, or, on the Application of the Legislatures of two thirds of the several States, shall call a Convention for proposing Amendments, which, in either Case, shall be valid to all Intents and Purposes, as Part of this Constitution, when ratified by the Legislatures of three fourths of the several States, or by Conventions in three fourths thereof, as the one or the other Mode of Ratification may be proposed by the Congress; Provided that no Amendment which may be made prior to the Year One thousand eight hundred and eight shall in any Manner affect the first and fourth Clauses in the Ninth Section of the first Article; and that no State, without its Consent, shall be deprived of its equal Suffrage in the Senate.

PROPOSED EQUAL RIGHTS AMENDMENT

Resolved by the Senate and House of Representatives of the United States of America in Congress assembled (two-thirds of each House concurring therein) that the following Article is proposed as an amendment to the Constitution of the United States, which shall be valid to all intents and purposes as part of the Constitution when ratified by the legislatures of three-fourths of the several States within seven years of the date of its submission by the Congress.

ARTICLE

1. Equality of rights under the law shall not be denied or abridged by the United States or by any State on account of sex.
2. The Congress shall have the power to enforce by appropriate legislation, the provisions of this article.
3. This amendment shall take effect two years after the date of ratification.

ARTICLE XIII.

Section 1. Neither slavery nor involuntary servitude, except as a punishment for crime whereof the party shall have been duly convicted, shall exist within the United States, or any place subject to their jurisdiction.

Section 2. Congress shall have power to enforce this article by appropriate legislation. [December 18, 1865.]

ARTICLE XIV.

Section 1. All persons born or naturalized in the United States, and subject to the jurisdiction thereof, are citizens of the United States and of the State wherein they reside. No State shall make or enforce any law which shall abridge the privileges or immunities of citizens of the United States: nor shall any State deprive any person of life, liberty, or property, without due process of law: nor deny to any person within its jurisdiction the equal protection of the laws.

Section 2. Representatives shall be apportioned among the several States according to their respective numbers, counting the whole number of persons in each State, excluding Indians not taxed. But when the right to vote at any election for the choice of electors for President and Vice President of the United States, Representatives in Congress, the Executive and Judicial officers of a State, or the members of the Legislature thereof, is denied to any of the male inhabitants of such State, being twenty-one years of age, and citizens of the United States, or in any way abridged, except for participation in rebellion, or other crime, the basis of representation therein shall be reduced in the proportion which the number of such male citizens shall bear to the whole number of male citizens twenty-one years of age in such State.

Section 3. No person shall be a Senator or Representative in Congress, or elector of President and Vice President, or hold any office, civil or military, under the United States, or under any State, who, having previously taken an oath, as a member of Congress, or as an officer of the United States, or as a member of any State legislature, or as an executive or judicial officer of any State, to support the Constitution of the United States, shall have engaged in insurrection or rebellion against the same, or given aid or comfort to the enemies thereof. But Congress may by a vote of two-thirds of each House, remove such disability.

Section 4. The validity of the public debt of the United States, authorized by law, including debts incurred for payment of pensions and bounties for services in suppressing insurrection or rebellion, shall not be questioned. But neither the United States nor any State shall assume or pay any debt or obligation incurred in aid of insurrection or rebellion against the United States, or any claim for the loss or emancipation of any slave: but all such debts, obligations and claims shall be held illegal and void.

Section 5. The Congress shall have power to enforce, by appropriate legislation, the provisions of this article. [July 28, 1868.]

ARTICLE XV.

Section 1. The right of citizens of the United States to vote shall not be denied or abridged by the United States or by any State on account of race, color, or previous condition of servitude—

Section 2. The Congress shall have power to enforce this article by appropriate legislation.—[March 30, 1870.]

ARTICLE XVI.

The Congress shall have power to lay and collect taxes on incomes, from whatever source derived, without apportionment among the several States, and without regard to any census or enumeration. [February 25, 1913.]

ARTICLE XVIII.

After one year from the ratification of this article, the manufacture, sale, or transportation of intoxicating liquors within, the importation thereof into, or the exportation thereof from the United States and all territory subject to the jurisdiction thereof for beverage purposes is hereby prohibited.

The Congress and the several States shall have concurrent power to enforce this article by appropriate legislation.

This article shall be inoperative unless it shall have been ratified as an amendment to the Constitution by the legislatures of the several States, as provided in the Constitution, within seven years from the date of the submission thereof to the States by Congress. [January 29, 1919.]

ARTICLE XIX.

The right of citizens of the United States to vote shall not be denied or abridged by the United States or by any State on account of sex.

The Congress shall have power by appropriate legislation to enforce the provisions of this article. [August 26, 1920.]

ARTICLE XXI.

Section 1. The eighteenth article of amendment to the Constitution of the United States is hereby repealed.

Section 2. The transportation or importation into any State, Territory or possession of the United States for delivery or use therein of intoxicating liquors, in violation of the laws thereof, is hereby prohibited.

Section 3. This article shall be inoperative unless it shall have been ratified as an amendment to the Constitution by convention in the several States, as provided in the Constitution, within seven years from the date of the submission thereof to the States by the Congress. [December 5, 1933.]

JOINT RESOLUTION PROPOSING AN AMENDMENT TO THE CONSTITUTION OF THE UNITED STATES

Resolved by the Senate and House of Representatives of the United States of America in Congress assembled (two-thirds of each House concurring therein), That the fol-

lowing article is proposed as an amendment to the Constitution of the United States, which, when ratified by the legislatures of three-fourths of the several States, shall be valid to all intents and purposes as a part of the Constitution:

ARTICLE —

Section 1. The Congress shall have power to limit, regulate, and prohibit the labor of persons under 18 years of age.

Section 2. The power of the several States is unimpaired by this article except that the operation of State laws shall be suspended to the extent necessary to give effect to legislation enacted by the Congress.

Notes

Introduction

1. *New York Times*, November 27, 1983, p. 1.
2. Marquerite Michaels, "The Myth of the Gender Gap," *Parade Magazine*, March 4, 1984, pp. 4–5.

1. The Early History of the Constitutional Amendment Process

1. George Mason at the Constitutional Convention noted that changes could be necessary, "better to provide for them in an easy, regular and Constitutional way than to trust to chance and violence," Max Farrand, *The Records of the Federal Convention of 1787* (New Haven: Yale University Press, 1911), vol. 1, pp. 202–203; Roger B. Traynor, "The Amendment System of the United States Constitution: An Historical and Legal Analysis (Ph.D. dissertation, University of California, Berkeley, 1927), pp. 85, 189–91, 204–205; Paul J. Scheips, "The Significance and Adoption of Article V of the Constitution," *Notre Dame Lawyer*, 26 (Fall 1951): 46; Constitution, Article V; Articles of Confederation, Article XIII; Walter F. Dellinger, "The Legislating of Constitutional Change: Rethinking the Amendment Process," 97 *Harvard Law Review* 386 (1983): 431 (Dellinger, while arguing against promulgation by Congress, asserts, "Article V does manifest concern with ensuring that consensus exists in favor of an amendment. This consensus is adequately addressed by the procedures Article V designates as the exclusive means of amending the Constitution" [p. 419]); Laurence Tribe, "A Constitution We Are Amending: In Defense of a Restrained Judicial Role," 97 *Harvard Law Review* (1983): 433.

2. Herman Ames, *The Proposed Amendments to the Constitution of the United States during the First Century of Its History*, Annual Report of the American Historical Association (1896), vol. II (Washington, D.C.: Government Printing Office, 1897), pp. 13–15; Lester B. Orfield, *The Amending of the Federal Constitution* (Chicago: Callaghan & Company, 1942), pp. 1–2; Jonathan Elliot, ed., *Debates on the Adoption of the Federal Constitution* (1941 facsimile of 1836 edition), vol. 5, pp. 123, 190.

3. Elliot, *Debates*, Vol. 5, pp. 157, 182; Orfield, *Amending the Constitution*, p. 2.

4. Elliot, *Debates*, vol. 5, pp. 190, 351, 376–81, 498, 530–32, 551–52, 553–67; Orfield, *Amending the Constitution*, pp. 4, 6; Ames, *The Proposed Amendments*, p. 17.

5. Orfield, *Amending the Constitution*, pp. 5–6; Ames, *The Proposed Amendments*, pp. 16–17; Jacob Cooke, ed., *The Federalist* (Middletown, CT: Wesleyan University Press, 1961), p. 296; no. 38.

6. *Current American Government, Spring 1983 Guide* (Congressional Quarterly, Inc.); Senate Document No. 82, 92d Cong., 2d sess., 1977, p. 51.

7. Cooke, ed., *The Federalist*, p. 578; no. 84; Elliot, *Debates*, vol. 5, p. 538.

8. Edward Dumbauld, *The Bill of Rights* (Norman: University of Oklahoma Press, 1957), pp. 30–32; Robert A. Rutland, *The Birth of the Bill of Rights* (Chapel Hill: University of North Carolina Press, 1955), pp. 131–33, 171; Ames, *Proposed Amendments*, p. 19; John Miller, *The Federalist Era, 1789–1801* (New York: Harper and Row, 1960), pp. 20–24.

9. Ames, *Proposed Amendments*, p. 26; Miller, *The Federalist Era*, p. 23.

10. Cooke, ed., *The Federalist*, p. 529; Ames, *Proposed Amendments*, pp. 156–57, 183–86; *Chisholm* v. *Georgia*, 2 Dallas 419 (1793); Miller, *The Federalist Era*, p. 180.

11. Ames, *Proposed Amendments*, pp. 19, 79.

12. Ibid. pp. 19–22, 186–89.

13. Don E. Fehrenbacher, *The Dred Scott Case in Historical Perspective* (New York: Oxford University Press, 1981), pp. 297–300; Mary Frances Berry, *Military Necessity and Civil Rights Policy, 1861–1868* (Port Washington, NY: Kennikat Press, 1977), pp. 85–93; *Dred Scott* v. *Sanford*, 19 Howard 393 (1857).

14. LaWanda Cox and John Cox, *Politics, Principle, and Prejudice, 1865–66* (New York; Free Press of Glencoe, 1963), p. 30; Berry, *Military Necessity*, pp. 85–86, 89.

15. William Gillette, *The Right to Vote: Politics and the Passage of the Fifteenth Amendment* (Baltimore: Johns Hopkins University Press, 1965), pp. 46–50; *Congressional Globe*, 40th Cong., 3d sess., Feb. 25, 1869, pp. 1563–64; 39th Cong., 1st sess., (June 8, 1866, 3149), p. 3042, (June 13, 1866), p. 3149; Michael Les Benedict, *A Compromise of Principle: Congressional Republicans and Reconstruction, 1863–1869* (New York: Norton Co., 1974), pp. 325–36.

2. Adopting an Income Tax

1. Herman Ames, *The Proposed Amendments to the Constitution of the United States during the First Century of Its History*, Annual Report of the American Historical Association (1896), vol. II (Washington, D.C.: Government Printing Office, 1897), pp. 242–45; Randolph E. Paul, *Taxation in the United States* (Boston: Little, Brown, 1954), pp. 1–3.

2. Paul, *Taxation*, pp. 4–5; Mary Frances Berry, *Military Necessity and Civil Rights Policy, 1861–1868* (Port Washington, NY: Kennikat Press, 1977), p. 14 and notes there cited.

3. Ames, *Proposed Amendments*, pp. 241–45; Paul, *Taxation*, pp. 4–7.

4. Paul, *Taxation*, pp. 7–17; Ray G. Blakey and Gladys C. Blakey, *The Federal Income Tax* (New York: Longmans, 1940), pp. 2–8.

5. Quoted in Paul, *Taxation*, pp. 22–29.

6. Paul, *Taxation*, p. 61; Blakey, *The Federal Income Tax*, p. 18; *Springer* v. *U.S.*, 102 U.S. 586 (1881).

7. Blakey, *The Federal Income Tax*, p. 89.

8. Blakey, *The Federal Income Tax*, pp. 10–12; Sherman Antitrust Act, vol. 26 U.S. *Statutes at Large* (1890) p. 209; William Letwin, *Law and Economic Policy in America: The Evolution of the Sherman Antitrust Act* (New York: Random House, 1965), pp. 67–8, 85–95.

9. Blakey , *The Federal Income Tax*, pp. 12–17.

10. Ibid. pp. 17–19; Paul, *Taxation*, pp. 40–54.

11. Blakey, *The Federal Income Tax*, pp. 17–19; Paul, *Taxation*, pp. 55–57; *Pollock* v. *Farmer's Loan and Trust Co.*, 157 U.S. 429 (1895).

12. Paul, *Taxation*, pp. 59–64; Blakey, *The Federal Income Tax*, pp. 19–20; *Pollock* v. *Farmer's Loan and Trust Co.*, rehearing, 158 U.S. 601 (1895).

13. Paul, *Taxation*, pp. 63–64; Blakey, *The Federal Income Tax*, pp. 20–21.

14. Paul, *Taxation*, pp. 86–88.

15. Blakey, *The Federal Income Tax*, pp. 20–21; Paul, *Taxation*, pp. 89–90.

16. Blakey, *The Federal Income Tax*, pp. 22–23; Paul, *Taxation*, pp. 90–91.

17. Paul, *Taxation*, pp. 90–99; Blakey, *The Federal Income Tax*, pp. 60–70; Alexander Bickel and Benno C. Schmidt, Jr., *The Judiciary and Responsible Government 1910–21*, vol. IV of *History of the Supreme Court of the United States* (New York: Macmillan Publishers, 1984), pp. 23–25.

18. Paul, *Taxation*, pp. 90–99; Blakey, *The Federal Income Tax*, pp. 60–70.

19. Gabriel Kolko, *Wealth and Power in America: An Analysis of Social Class and Income Distribution* (London: Thames & Hudson, 1962), pp. 30—45; Holmes quote from *Compania de Tabacos* v. *Collector*, 275 U.S. 87, 100 (1904); Jerold L. Waltman, *Political Origins of the Income Tax* (Jackson: University Press of Mississippi, 1985), discusses the earliest revenue acts passed under the authority of the Sixteenth Amendment.

20. Paul, *Taxation*, pp. 91, 92, 97, 101, 102; Blakey, *The Federal Income Tax*, pp. 64, 68–69; John D. Buenker, "The Adoption of the Income Tax Amendment: A Case Study of a Progressive Reform" (Ph.D. dissertation, Georgetown University, 1964).

21. Kolko, *Wealth and Power*, chapter 2.

22. *New York Times*, August 20, 1983, p. 12; "Income Tax Compliance, Revenue Estimates for 1973–1981, July 1983, Internal Revenue Service, The Legal Section, Tax Gap Reported and Unreported Income" (information obtained by author from IRS by telephone, unpublished IRS report).

3. Generating an Artificial Consensus

1. Andrew Sinclair, *Prohibition: The Era of Excess* (Boston: Little, Brown, 1962) pp. 36–37; David E. Kyvig, *Repealing National Prohibition* (Chicago: University of Chicago Press, 1979) p. 200.

2. John Krout, *The Origins of Prohibition* (New York: A. Knopf, 1925), p. 183; Sinclair, *Prohibition*, pp. 36–38; Ruth Bordin, *Woman and Temperance: The Quest for Power and Liberty, 1873–1900* (Philadelphia: Temple University Press, 1981), p. 4. Ian R. Tyrell, *Sobering Up: From Temperance to Prohibition in Antebellum America, 1800–1860* (Westport, CT: Greenwood Press, 1979), pp. 54–86.

3. Sinclair, *Prohibition*, pp. 83–84; D. Leigh Colvin, *The Prohibition Party in the United States* (New York: George H. Doran & Co., 1926), pp. 53–54, 147; Herbert Asbury, *The Great Illusion: An Informal History of Prohibition* (Westport, CT: Greenwood Press, 1968 [1950]), pp. 88–95.

4. Sinclair, *Prohibition*, pp. 84–85; Peter H. Odegard, *Pressure Politics: The Story of the Anti-Saloon League* (New York: Columbia University Press, 1928), pp. 80–84.

5. Sinclair, *Prohibition*, pp. 85–89; Odegard, *Pressure Politics*, pp. 6, 9–10, 97, 120–21, 182; David E. Kyvig, "Amending the U.S. Constitution: Ratification Controversies, 1917–1971," *Ohio History*, vol. 83 (Summer 1974): 156–59.

6. Sinclair, *Prohibition*, pp. 90–91.

7. Perry R. Duis, *The Saloon: Public Drinking in Chicago and Boston, 1880–1920* (Urbana: University of Illinois Press, 1983), 110–113, 123–42.

8. Jed Dannenbaum, *Drink and Disorder: Temperance Reform in Connecticut from the Washington Revival to the WCTU* (Urbana: University of Illinois Press, 1984), pp. 181–82; Sinclair, *Prohibition*, pp. 91–92; Bordin, *Woman and Tem-*

perance, pp. 4–6; Frederick Luebke, *Immigrants and Politics: The Germans of Nebraska* (Lincoln: University of Nebraska, 1969), p. 129.

9. Jed Dannenbaum, "The Origin of Temperance Activism and Militancy Among American Women," *Journal of Social History* 15(1981–82): 235–252; Sinclair, *Prohibition*, pp. 93–96; Bordin, *Woman and Temperance*, pp. 15–52.

10. Sinclair, *Prohibition*, pp. 96–97; David Morgan, *Suffragists and Democrats: The Politics of Woman Suffrage in America* (East Lansing: Michigan State University Press, 1972), pp. 107–113.

11. Odegard, *Pressure Politics*, p. 95; Jack S. Blocker, *Retreat from Reform: The Prohibition Movement in the U.S., 1890–1913* Westport, CT: Greenwood Press, 1976), pp.164–66; Ella Alexander Boole, *Give Prohibition Its Chance* (Evanston, IL: National Women's Christian Temperance Union Publishing House, 1929), pp. 66–68.

12. Sinclair, *Prohibition*,. pp. 60–62; Joseph Gusfield, *Symbolic Crusade: Status Politics and the American Temperance Movement* (Westport, CT: Greenwood Press, 1980 reprint; originally published by University of Illinois Press, 1963), p. 117.

13. Sinclair, *Prohibition*, pp. 114–26; Paul E. Isaac, *Prohibition and Politics: Turbulent Decades in Tennessee, 1885–1920* (Knoxville: University of Tennessee Press, 1965), pp. 257–58.

14. Sinclair, *Prohibition*, p. 126.

15. Sinclair, *Prohibition*, p. 154; *Congressional Record*, 62d Cong., 3d sess., 1913, pp. 761, 2824, 2836, 2867–68, 4297–99.

16. Sinclair, *Prohibition*, p. 29, 48, 154, 155, 156–57; Isaac, *Prohibition and Politics*, p. 266.

17. Sinclair, *Prohibition*, pp. 162–63; Odegard, *Pressure Politics*, pp. 153–74; Blocker, *Retreat from Reform*, pp. 239–44; James H. Timberlake, *Prohibition and the Progressive Movement, 1900–1920* (Cambridge: Harvard University Press, 1963), pp. 170–73.

18. Sinclair, *Prohibition*, p. 164; Odegard, *Pressure Politics*, pp. 174–80.

19. Sinclair, *Prohibition*, p. 166; *Rhode Island* v. *Palmer*, 253 U.S. 350 (1920).

20. Sinclair, *Prohibition*, pp. 166–70, 173–220, 390, 392; Kyvig, *Repealing National Prohibition*, pp. 197–99; Sean Dennis Cashman, *Prohibition: The Lie of the Land* (New York: Free Press, 1981), pp. 218–21.

21. Kyvig, *Repealing National Prohibition*, pp. 45, 91–95, 143, 190–95; Grace C. Root, *Women and Repeal, The Story of the Women's Organization for National Prohibition Reform* (New York: Harper & Bros., 1934), pp. 161–62.

22. Sinclair, *Prohibition*, pp. 390, 392; Kyvig, *Repealing Prohibition*, pp. 200–201.

23. Gusfield, *Symbolic Crusade*, pp. 126–29. Norman Clark, *Deliver Us from Evil, An Interpretation of American Prohibition* (New York: Norton, 1976), and Bordin, *Woman and Temperance*, p. xv, emphasize more than Gusfield the seriousness of alcohol abuse, but admitting the seriousness does not mean that a consensus existed to outlaw drinking.

4. Gaining Woman Suffrage

1. Andrew Sinclair, *The Emancipation of the American Woman* (New York: Harper & Row, 1965), pp. 30–32; Eleanor Flexner, *Century of Struggle: The Woman's Rights Movement in the United States* (Cambridge: Harvard University Press, 1959, 1972), pp. 143–44.

2. Sinclair, *Emancipation*, pp. 84–90; Leo Kanowitz, *Women and the Law: The Unfinished Revolution* (Albuquerque: University of New Mexico Press,

1969), pp. 35–41; David Morgan, *Suffragists and Democrats: The Politics of Woman Suffrage in America* (East Lansing: Michigan State University Press, 1972), p. 41; Carl Degler, *At Odds: Women and the Family in America from the Revolution to the Present* (New York: Oxford University Press, 1980), pp. 342–50; Flexner, *Century of Struggle*, pp. 71–77.

3. Ellen DuBois, *Feminism and Suffrage: The Emergence of an Independent Women's Movement in America* (Ithaca, NY: Cornell University Press, 1978), pp. 53–64; Flexner, *Century of Struggle*, pp. 110–11, 144–45; Mary Frances Berry, *Military Necessity and Civil Rights Policy: Black Citizenship and the Constitution, 1861–1868* (Port Washington, NY: Kennikat Press, 1977), pp. 92–95.

4. Aileen S. Kraditor, *Ideas of the Woman Suffrage Movement, 1890–1920* (New York: Columbia University Press, 1965), pp. 131, 172, 213; Flexner, *Century of Struggle*, p. 220; DuBois, *Feminism and Suffrage*, p. 178. On racism in the suffrage movement generally, see Paula Giddings, *When and Where I Enter: The Impact of Black Women on Race and Sex in America* (New York: Morrow Co., 1984), pp. 119–31, 159–70; Angela Y. Davis, *Women, Race, and Class* (New York: Random House, 1981), pp. 109–26; Rosalyn Terborg-Penn, "Afro-Americans in the Struggle for Woman Suffrage" (Ph.D. dissertation, Howard University, 1977).

5. DuBois, *Feminism and Suffrage*, pp. 164–75; Flexner, *Century of Struggle*, pp. 152–53.

6. Flexner, *Century of Struggle*, pp.148–49, 174–75; Herman Ames, *The Proposed Amendments to the Constitution of the United States during the First Century of Its History*, Annual Report of the American Historical Association (1896), vol.II (Washington, D.C.: Government Printing office, 1897), pp. 237–38.

7. William O'Neill, *Everyone Was Brave: The Rise and Fall of Feminism in America* (Chicago: Quadrangle Books, 1969), pp. 25–31; Flexner, *Century of Struggle*, p. 154; Sinclair, *Emancipation*, pp. 191–93.

8. Sinclair, *Emancipation*, pp. 193–95; Flexner, *Century of Struggle*, pp. 167–69, 175; Elisabeth Griffin, *In Her Own Right: The Life of Elizabeth Cady Stanton* (New York: Oxford University Press, 1983), p. 154.

9. Sinclair, *Emancipation*, p. 195; *Minor v. Happersett*, 21 Wallace 162 (1875); Flexner, *Century of Struggle*, pp. 168–70.

10. Sinclair, *Emancipation*, pp. 172–73.

11. Sinclair, *Emancipation*, pp. 293–94; Flexner, *Century of Struggle*, pp. 216–20; Kraditor, *Ideas of the Woman Suffrage Movement*, p. 4.

12. Flexner, *Century of Struggle*, pp. 221, 237–39, 249; Kraditor, *Ideas of the Woman Suffrage Movement*, pp. 163–66.

13. Sinclair, *Emancipation*, pp. 208–12; Flexner, *Century of Struggle*, pp. 177–78; Miriam Chapman, "The Story of Woman Suffrage in Wyoming, 1869–1890" (MA thesis, University of Wyoming, 1952); Julie R. Jeffrey, *Frontier Women: The Trans-Mississippi West, 1840–1880* (New York: Hill and Wang, 1979), pp. 190–93; Glenda Riley, *Women and Indians on the Frontier, 1825–1915* (Albuquerque: University of New Mexico Press, 1984), p. 13.

14. Flexner, *Century of Struggle*, pp. 162–63, 212–15; Jeffrey, *Frontier Women*, p. 190.

15. Sinclair, *Emancipation*, pp. 216–17; Flexner, *Century of Struggle*, pp. 222–23.

16. Flexner, *Century of Struggle*, pp. 222–24, 217–19.

17. Sinclair, *Emancipation*, pp. 222–23; Flexner, *Century of Struggle*, pp. 181–85; Janet Giele, "Social Change in the Woman Suffrage Movement, 1890–1920" (Ph.D. dissertation, Columbia University, 1962).

18. Sinclair, *Emancipation*, pp. 223–28; Flexner, *Century of Struggle*, pp. 185–86; Kraditor, *Ideas of the Woman Suffrage Movement*, pp. 162–83; David Morgan, *Suffragists and Democrats*, pp. 158–66.

19. Sinclair, *Emancipation*, pp. 227, 229; Lauren Kessler, "A Siege of the Citadels: Search for a Public Forum for the Ideas of Oregon Woman Suffrage," 84 *Oregon Historical Quarterly* (1983): 117–49; Flexner, *Century of Struggle*, pp. 151–53; O'Neill, *Everyone Was Brave*, pp. 18–24, 33–38; Kraditor, *Ideas of the Woman Suffrage Movement*, pp. 110–31.

20. Sinclair, *Emancipation*, pp. 324–26; Flexner, *Century of Struggle*, pp. 249, 262.

21. Flexner, *Century of Struggle*, pp. 221, 237–39, 249; Kraditor, *Ideas of the Woman Suffrage Movement*, pp. 163, 166.

21. Flexner, *Century of Struggle*, pp. 298–302, 249–52; 258–59.

22. Flexner, *Century of Struggle*, pp. 302–303, 263–64; Susan D. Becker, *The Origins of the Equal Rights Amendment: American Feminism Between the Wars* (Westport, CT: Greenwood Press, 1981), pp. 44–48.

23. Flexner, *Century of Struggle*, pp. 267–74; Morgan, *Suffragists and Democrats*, pp. 92–95.

24. Flexner, *Century of Struggle*, p. 303.

25. Sinclair, *Emancipation*, pp. 303–304, 326; Flexner, *Century of Struggle*, p. 269.

26. Sinclair, *Emancipation*, pp. 328–30; Flexner, *Century of Struggle*, pp. 276–77.

27. Sinclair, *Emancipation*, p. 331; Flexner, *Century of Struggle*, pp. 305–15.

28. Sinclair, *Emancipation*, pp. 331–34; Flexner, *Century of Struggle*, pp. 278–79, 288–290; Sidney Roderick Bland, "Techniques of Persuasion: The National Woman's Party and Woman Suffrage, 1913–1919" (Ph.D. dissertation, George Washington University, 1977).

29. Sinclair, *Emancipation*, pp. 331–39; Flexner, *Century of Struggle*, pp. 291–93; Lemons, *The Woman Citizen: Social Feminism in the 1920's* (Urbana: University of Illinois Press, 1973), p. 29; Flexner, *Century of Struggle*, pp. 240, 242, 311–13.

30. *Leser v. Garnett*, 258 U.S. 130 (1922); William L. Marbury, "The 19th Amendment and After," 7 *University of Virginia Law Review* (October 1920): 1–29.

31. Rosalyn Terborg-Penn, "Discrimination Against Afro-American Women in the Woman's Movement, 1830–1920," in Sharon Harley and Rosalyn Terborg-Penn, eds., *The Afro-American Woman: Struggles and Images* (Port Washington, NY: Kennikat Press, 1978), pp. 17–28; Paula Giddings, *When and Where I Enter: The Impact of Black Women on Race and Sex in America* (New York: Morrow Co., 1984), pp. 127–28; Nancy Cott, "Feminist Politics in the 1920's: The National Woman Party," 71 *Journal of American History* (1984): 50–54; Kraditor, *Ideas of the Woman Suffrage Movement*, p. 213; Rosalyn Terborg-Penn, "Discontented Black Feminists: Prelude and Postscripts to the Nineteenth Amendment," in Lois Scharf and Jan M. Jackson, eds., *Decades of Discontent: The Women's Movement, 1920–1940* (Westport, CT: Greenwood Press, 1983).

32. Virginia, North Carolina, South Carolina, Georgia, Alabama, Louisiana, Mississippi, and Florida ratified neither the Nineteenth Amendment nor ERA. Maryland and Delaware did not ratify the Nineteenth Amendment, but did ratify ERA.

5. Social Reform between the Wars

1. J. Stanley Lemons, *The Woman Citizen: Social Feminism in the 1920's* (Urbana: University of Illinois Press, 1973), pp. 16, 17, 32; Susan D. Becker, *The Origins of the Equal Rights Amendment: American Feminism Between the Wars* (Westport, CT: Greenwood Press, 1981), p. 128.

2. Lemons, *The Woman Citizen*, chapter 6; William Chafe, *The American Woman: Her Changing Social, Economic, and Political Roles, 1920–1970* (New York: Oxford University Press, 1972), pp. 27–28; Stephen Wood, *Constitutional Politics in the Progressive Era: Child Labor and the Law* (Chicago: University of Chicago Press, 1968), pp. 3–5; David Morgan, *Suffragists and Democrats, The Politics of Woman Suffrage in America* (East Lansing: Michigan State University Press, 1972), pp. 165–77; Caroline F. Ware, *The Early New England Cotton Manufacture: A Study in Industrial Beginnings* (Boston: Houghton-Mifflin, 1934), pp. 199–200, 210–11; Jack Blicksilver, *Cotton Manufacturing in the Southeast: An Historical Analysis* (Atlanta: Bureau of Business and Economic Research, School of Business Administration, Georgia State College of Business Administration, 1959), pp. 28–29.

3. Lela B. Costin, "Women and Physicians: The 1930 White House Conference on Children," *Journal of the National Association of Social Workers*, vol. 28 (March-April 1983): 108–115; Lemons, *The Woman Citizen*, chapter 6; *Massachusetts* v. *Mellon* and *Frothingham* v. *Mellon*, 262 U.S. 447 (1923).

4. Alonzo McLaurin Mellin, "The Southern Cotton Textile Operative and Organized Labor, 1880–1905 (Ph.D. dissertation, University of South Carolina, 1967).

5. Wood, *Constitutional Politics*, pp. 6–10.

6. Ibid., pp. 10–13.

7. Ibid., pp. 13–17.

8. Ibid.

9. *Lochner* v. *New York*, 198 U.S. 45 (1905); *Muller* v. *Oregon*, 208 U.S. 402 (1908); Chafe, *The American Woman*, pp. 80, 128–29; Wood, *Constitutional Politics*, pp. 20–21.

10. Raymond G. Fuller, "Progress in Standards of Child Labor Legislation," *Proceedings of the National Conference of Social Work*, 49th Annual Session (1922) (Chicago: University of Chicago Press, 1922), pp. 281–84; Wood, *Constitutional Politics*, pp. 22–24.

11. See, for example, *McCray* v. *United States*, 195 U.S. 27 (1904), use of the taxing power to regulate oleomargarine; *Champion* v. *Ames*, 188 U.S. 321 (1902), use of the commerce power to outlaw lotteries; *Hoke* v. *United States*, 27 U.S. 308 (1913), outlawing interstate traffic in prostitution; Wood, *Constitutional Politics*, pp. 26–31.

12. Wood, *Constitutional Politics*, pp. 31–42, 55–58, 75–78.

13. *Hammer* v. *Dagenhart*, 247 U.S. 251 (1918).

14. Wood, *Constitutional Politics*, pp. 185–88, 193–94.

15. Ibid., pp. 195–208, 215–16.

16. Fuller, "Progress in Standards," pp. 281–84; Lemons, *The Woman Citizen*, pp. 144–45.

17. Wood, *Constitutional Politics*, pp. 220–23, 225, 228.

18. *Bailey* v. *Drexel Furniture Company*, 259 U.S. 20 (1922); Wood, *Constitutional Politics*, pp. 260–80.

19. Lemons, *The Woman Citizen*, pp. 208–13; Josephine Goldmark, *Impatient Crusader* (Urbana: University of Illinois Press, 1953), pp. 114–20; Clement E.

Vose, *Constitutional Change: Amendment Politics and Supreme Court Litigation Since 1900* (Lexington, MA: D.C. Heath, 1972), pp. 249–51.

20. Lemons, *The Woman Citizen*, pp. 214–15.
21. Ibid., pp. 160, 214–15, 219.
22. Ibid., p. 220.
23. Ibid., pp. 221–25.
24. Ibid., p. 147.
25. *U.S.* v. *Darby Lumber Co.*, 312 U.S. 100 (1941); Lemons, *The Woman Citizen*, pp. 297–99; Vose, *Constitutional Change*, pp. 351–52.

6. ERA: Approval and Early Ratification Campaigns

1. J. Stanley Lemons, *Woman Citizen: Social Feminism in the 1920's* (Urbana: University of Illinois Press, 1973), pp. 16–17, 32, chapter 6; Susan Becker, *The Origins of the Equal Rights Amendment: American Feminism Between the Wars* (Westport, CT: Greenwood Press, 1981), pp. 128–30.
2. Susan Ware, *Holding Their Own: American Women in the 1930's* (Boston: Twayne Publishers, 1982), pp. 89–94; Elsie George, "The Women Appointees of the Roosevelt and Truman Administrations: A Study of Their Impact and Effectiveness" (Ph.D. dissertation, American University, 1972); William Chafe, *The American Woman: Her Changing Social, Economic, and Political Roles, 1920–1970* (New York: Oxford University Press, 1972), pp. 42, 112–13, 127–28; Nancy F. Cott, "Feminist Politics in the 1920's: The National Woman's Party," 71 *Journal of American History* (June 1984): 43–68, 59.
3. *Muller* v. *Oregon*, 208 U.S. 412 (1908); *Adkins* v. *Children's Hospital*, 261 U.S. 525 (1923); Ware, *Holding Their Own*, pp. 21–30. Chafe, *The American Woman*, pp. 49–61, 127–28, emphasizes declines in employment and prevalence of traditional attitudes toward outside the home work; but see Winifred D. Wandersee, "The Economics of Middle Income Family Life: Working Women During the Great Depression," 65 *Journal of American History* (June 1978): 60–74.
4. Chafe, *The American Woman*, pp. 88–111; Ware, *Holding Their Own*, pp. 66–69.
5. Chafe, *The American Woman*, pp. 130–31; Ware, *Holding Their Own*, pp. 107–11.
6. Chafe, *The American Woman*, pp. 135–50; Becker, *The Origins of the Equal Rights Amendment*, pp. 18–22.
7. Ethel Beer, *Working Mothers and the Day Nursery* (Mystic, CT: Lawrence Verry Inc., 1970), pp. 27–40; Mary Bogue and Mary Moran, "Day Nurseries," *Social Work Yearbook*, vol. 1 (1929): 118–19; Allen F. Davis, *Spearheads for Reformers: The Social Settlements and the Progressive Movement, 1890–1914* (New York: Oxford University Press, 1967), pp. 43–46; Valerie Oppenheimer, *The Female Labor Force in the United States: Demographic and Economic Factors Governing Its Growth and Changing Composition* (Berkeley: University of California Press, 1970), pp. 36–37, 47–51; Chafe, *The American Woman*, pp. 164–65; Rosalyn F. Baxandall, "Who Shall Care for Our Children? The History and Development of Day Care in the United States," in Jo Freeman, ed., *Women: A Feminist Perspective* (Palo Alto, CA: Mayfield Publishing Co., 1975, 1979), pp. 135–38.
8. Chafe, *The American Woman*, pp. 160–72; Baxandall, "Who Shall Care for Our Children?" pp. 138–39.
9. 96 *Congressional Record*, 81st Cong., 2d sess., 1950, pp. 861–73; 99 *Congressional Record*, 83d Cong.) 1st sess., 1953, pp. 8951–74.

10. Mary Frances Berry and John W. Blassingame, *Long Memory: The Black Experience in America* (New York: Oxford University Press, 1982), pp. 83–92; Pauline Terrelonge Stone, "Feminist Consciousness and Black Women," in Freeman, ed., *Women: A Feminist Perspective*, pp. 575–86; Susan Estabrook Kennedy, *If All We Did was to Weep at Home: A History of White Working Class Women in America* (Bloomington: Indiana University Press, 1979), pp. 220–24, 232; Kennedy, *If All We Did was to Weep*, pp. 220–40; Paula Giddings, *When and Where I Enter: The Impact of Black Women on Race and Sex in America* (New York: Morrow Co., 1984), pp. 250–58.

11. Chafe, *The American Woman*, pp. 200–24; Andrew Sinclair, *The Emancipation of the American Woman* (New York: Harper & Row, 1965), pp. 347–48.

12. Ware, *Holding Their Own*, pp. 16–17; Betty Friedan, *The Feminine Mystique* (New York: W.W. Norton Co., 1963); see also, Friedan, *It Changed My Life: Writings on the Women's Movement* (New York: Random House, 1963), part 1.

13. Emily George, *Martha L. Griffiths* (Lanham, MD: University Press of America, 1983), pp. 149–50, quoting from Griffiths, "Women and the Legislators," article written for the Unitarian Universalist Women's Federation, accompanied by letter; Griffiths to Mary Lou Thompson, March 20, 1970, Griffiths Personal Library, Romeo, Michigan; Griffiths to Caroline Bird, February 6, 1968, in Griffiths' Papers, Bentley Library, Ann Arbor, Michigan, Michigan Historical Collection.

14. Jo Freeman, *The Politics of Women's Liberation: A Case Study of an Emerging Social Movement and Its Relation to the Social Policy Process* (New York: Longman, 1975), pp. 53–55; Friedan, *It Changed My Life*, pp. 76–86; C. Berger, "Equal Pay, Employment Opportunity and Equal Enforcement of the Law for Women," 5 *Valparaiso Law Review* 327 (1971); Donald A. Robinson, "Two Movements in Pursuit of Equal Employment Opportunity," *Signs, Journal of Women in Culture and Society*, 4 (1979): 413–33.

15. Chafe, *The American Woman*, pp. 237–40.

16. Ibid., pp. 237–41.

17. *Reed v. Reed*, 404 U.S. 71 (1971); U.S. President's Commission on the Status of Women, *American Woman* (Washington, D.C., 1963); Cynthia E. Harrison, "A 'New Frontier' for Women: The Public Policy of the Kennedy Administration." *Journal of American History*, 67 (1980): 630–46.

18. Janet K. Boles, *The Politics of the Equal Rights Amendment: Conflict and the Decision Process* (New York: Longman, 1979), pp. 37–39; U.S. Congress, House, 92d Cong., 1st sess., 12 October 1971; H.R. Rep. No. 92–259, House Judiciary Committee, 92d Cong., 1st sess., (1971); 117 *Congressional Record*, H9392 (daily edition, Oct. 12, 1971).

19. S. Rep. No. 92–689, Senate Committee on the Judiciary, 92d Cong., 2d sess. (1972); 118 *Congressional Record*, S4247–4272 (daily edition, March 20, 1972); S4372–4430 (daily edition, March 21, 1972); S4531–4613 (daily edition March 22, 1972); Boles, *The Politics of the Equal Rights Amendment*, pp. 39–49.

20. Barbara Brown et al., "The Equal Rights Amendment: A Constitutional Basis for Equal Rights for Women," 80 *Yale Law Journal* (1971): 871–985, 884.

21. Lester Orfield, *The Amending of the Federal Constitution* (Chicago: Callaghan & Company, 1942), pp. 74–75; *Spring 1983 Guide, Current American Government* (Congressional Quarterly, Inc., 1983), pp. 3–4. (Some feminist

leaders recognized the mistake in accepting the deadline. See for example, Gloria Steinem, *Outrageous Acts and Everyday Rebellions* (New York: Holt, Rinehart & Winston, 1983), p. 348.); Boles, *The Politics of the Equal Rights Amendment*, p. 61.

22. Ross, "Sex Discrimination and Protective Labor Legislation," printed in Hearings on Section 805 of H.R. 16098 Before the Special Subcommittee on Education of the House Committee on Education and Labor, 91st Cong., 2d sess., at 592, 595–96 (1970). Materials cited in Brown et al., "The Equal Rights Amendment," p. 923, fn 99.

23. Carl N. Degler, *At Odds: Women and the Family in America from the Revolution to the Present* (New York: Oxford University Press, 1980), pp. 446–47; Boles, *The Politics of the Equal Rights Amendment*, pp. 61–62.

24. Boles, *The Politics of the Equal Rights Amendment*, pp. 4–5.

25. Ibid., pp. 7–8.

26. Ibid., pp. 21–24.

27. Ibid., pp. 67–70; Carol Felsenthal, *The Biography of Phyllis Schlafly, The Sweetheart of the Silent Majority* (Chicago: Regnery Gateway, 1982; originally published by Doubleday, 1981), pp. 232–41; interview with Phyllis Schlafly, June 11, 1985, Washington, D.C.

28. Boles, *The Politics of the Equal Rights Amendment*, pp. 62–63.

29. Ibid., pp. 64–66.

30. Giddings, *When and Where I Enter*, p. 347.

31. Val Burns, "Who Opposed the ERA? An Analysis of the Social Bases of Anti-Feminism," *Social Science Quarterly*, vol. 64 (1983): 305–18; Boles, *The Politics of the Equal Rights Amendment*, pp. 80–81; Kent L. Tedin et al., "Social Backgrounds and Political Differences Between Pro and Anti-ERA Activists," *American Political Quarterly*, vol. 5 (July 1977): 395–408.

32. Boles, *The Politics of the Equal Rights Amendment*, pp. 181–82. Schlafly describes the proponents' mood as displaying a psychology of inevitable victory, while she knew as soon as questions were raised about federal power, traditional family roles, abortion, and combat, that she would win. Interview with Phyllis Schlafly, June 11, 1985, Washington, D.C.

33. Boles, *The Politics of the Equal Rights Amendment*, pp. 176–78.

7. ERA: Extension, Rescission, and Failure

1. H.J. Res. 124 *Congressional Record*, H8664–65 (daily edition, August 15, 1978); 124 *Congressional Record*, S17318–19 (daily edition, October 6, 1978).

2. Grover Rees III, "Throwing Away the Key: The Unconstitutionality of the Equal Rights Amendment Extension," *58 Texas Law Rev.* (1980): 875–932; see also materials included in 124 *Congressional Record* S16659–64, (daily edition, Sept. 29, 1978) with the exception of a letter from Professor Herbert Wechsler to Rep. Don Edwards (Feb. 13, 1978).

3. Ruth Bader Ginsburg, "Ratification of the Equal Rights Amendment: A Question of Time," 57 *Texas Law Rev.* (1979): 919, 920; Comment: "ERA: The Effect of Extending the Time for Ratification on Attempts to Rescind Prior Ratifications," 128 *Emory L.J.* 71 (1979); Comment: "The Equal Rights Amendment and Article V: A Framework for Analysis of the Extension and Rescission Issues," 127 *U. Pa. L. Rev.* 494 (1978); Equal Rights Amendment Extension: Hearings on H.J. Res. 638 Before the Subcommittee on Civil and Constitutional Rights of the House Committee on the Judiciary, 95th Cong., 1st & 2d sess., 5–38 (1977–78), 39–59, 61–97, 115–56, 121–56; Equal Rights

Amendment Extension: Hearings on S.J. Res. 134 Before the Subcommittee on the Constitution of the Senate Committee on the Judiciary, 95th Cong., 2d Sess., 54–80 (1978).

4. *Coleman* v. *Miller*, 307 U.S. 433 (1939).

5. Robert Rutland et al., eds., *The Papers of James Madison*, 14 vols. (Charlottesville: University of Virginia Press, 1977), vol. II, p. 189, July 20, 1788 Letter to Alexander Hamilton.

6. See, for example, Senator Jake Garn (R, Wyo.), 124 *Congressional Record* S17,292–3 (daily edition, October 6, 1978).

7. Message of Governor Bramlette, quoted in John Alexander Jameson, *A Treatise on Constitutional Conventions; Their History, Powers and Modes of Proceeding*, 4th ed. (1887; reprint, New York: Da Capo Press, 1972), sec. 581; *White* v. *Hart*, 80 U.S. (13 Wall) 646 (1871); Comment: "ERA: The Effect of Extending the Time for Ratification on Attempts to Rescind Prior to Ratification," 28 *Emory Law Journal* (1979) 71–110, 78–84 and notes there cited.

8. S. Rep. No. 293, 93d Cong., 1st sess., 1973, "ERA: The Effect of Extending the Time," pp. 78–82.

9. *Hawke* v. *Smith*, 253 U.S. 221 (1920).

10. Jules Gerard, Professor of Law, Washington University, St. Louis, 124 *Congressional Record* E3,533 (daily edition, June 29, 1978); noted in "ERA: The Effect of Extending the Time," p. 101.

11. *Idaho* v. *Freeman*, 529 F. Supp. 1107, 1146, 1152–3 (1981), *judgment stayed*, Jan. 25, 1982, 102 S.Ct. 1272, 11; *Dyer* v. *Blair*, 390 F. Supp., 241 (N.D. Ill 1975); *Coleman* v. *Miller*, 307 U.S. 433, 59 S.Ct. 972, 183 L.Ed. 1885 (1939); *Baker* v. *Carr*, 369 U.S. 186, 214 (1962); *Powell* v. *McCormack*, 395 U.S. 486, 546–49 (1967). Grover Rees III, who served as special counsel to Senator Garn, floor leader of the opposition to extension, and was counsel for plaintiff intervenors in *Idaho* v. *Freeman*, discusses the issues in "Throwing Away the Key: The Unconstitutionality of the Equal Rights Amendment Extension," 58 *Texas L.Rev.* (1980): 875–931.

12. *Idaho* v. *Freeman*, 529 F.Supp. 1107, 1146, 1152–3 (1981), *judgment stayed* January 25, 1982, 102 S.Ct. 1272.

13. Janet K. Boles, *The Politics of the Equal Rights Amendment: Conflict and the Decision Process* (New York: Longman, 1979), pp. 2–3, 21.

14. Betty Friedan, *The Second Stage* (New York: Summit Books, Simon and Schuster, 1981), pp. 18–19, 24. When ERA failed the first time in Illinois, when the state rescissions began and finally when proponents needed an extension, Schlafly became increasingly convinced that ERA was dead. Interview with Phyllis Schlafly, June 11, 1985, Washington, D.C.

15. *New York Times*, February 9, pp. 1, 8; June 19, p. 18; June 20, p. 12; June 21, p. 8; August 27, p. 12; June 25, Sec. III, p. 21. Excitement was generated in Illinois by the charge and later conviction of NOW members for attempting to bribe a legislator to obtain his vote. *New York Times*, August 23, p. 2.

16. Friedan, *The Second Stage*, pp. 22–26.

17. Ibid., pp. 257–80, 326–30; Donald G. Matthews and Jane DeHart Matthews, "The Culture Politics of ERA's Defeat," *Newsletter*, Organization of American Historians, (1983); Carl Degler, *At Odds: Women and the Family in America from the Revolution to the Present* (New York: Oxford University Press, 1980), pp. 450–73.

18. *New York Times*, July 2, 1980, p. A16; July 8, 1980, p. 1, B8; July 10, 1980, p. 1, B18; July 11, 1980, p. 10.

19. *Washington Post*, January 23, 1981, p. 10; February 7, 1981, B5; *New York Times*, April 8, 1981, p. A20.

20. *Washington Post*, May 8, 1981, A13; *New York Times*, May 8, 1981, A16.

21. *New York Times*, May 15, 1981, A20; *New York Times*, July 1, 1981 (picture of rally was on p. 1); *Washington Post*, July 1, 1981, B8.

22. *Rostker* v. *Goldberg*, 453 U.S 57 (1980); *Craig* v. *Boren*, 429 U.S. 190 (1976); *McCarty* v. *McCarty*, 453 U.S. 210 (1981); *New York Times*, July 1, 1981, p. 1; *Washington Post*, June 27, 1981, A4.

23. Rosalyn Terborg-Penn, "Discrimination Against Afro-American Women in the Women's Movement, 1830–1920" in *The Afro-American Woman: Struggles and Images*, Sharon Harley and Rosalyn Terborg-Penn, eds. (Port Washington, N.Y.: Kennikat Press, 1978), pp 17–27; Bella Hooks, *Ain't I a Woman? Black Women and Feminism* (Boston: South End Press, 1981), p. 146; Thornton Dill, "Race, Class and Gender: Prospects for an All Inclusive Sisterhood," 9 *Feminist Studies* (Spring 1983): 131–50 and notes there cited.

24. *New York Times*, June 19, 1981, p. B4.

25. *Tallahassee Democrat*, July 19, 1981.

26. *Washington Post*, August 9, 1981, p. A3; August 23, 1981, p. B1. *New York Times*, August 23, 1981; picture on p. 1 of Betty Ford and Bradley; story on p. 29, first section.

27. *Washington Post*, November 6, 1983, B1; *Wall Street Journal*, November 13, 1981; *New York Times*, October 10, 1981, p. 18; *Washington Post*, October 13, 1981, B1.

28. *Washington Post*, January 10, 1982, p. 10.

29. *Washington Post*, January 10, 1982, p. 10.

30. *Washington Post*: January 13, 1982, p. 2; January 14, 1982, p. A3; January 19, 1982, p. A2; January 19, 1982, p. B1; January 20, 1982, p. A6; January 21, 1982, p. A4.

31. *Idaho* v. *Freeman*, 520 F.Supp. 1107, 1146, 1152–3 (1981), *judgment stayed*, January 25, 1982, 102 S.Ct. 1272; *Wall Street Journal*, December 24, 1981, p. 3; *Washington Post*, December 24, 1981, A6, p. 1; *New York Times*, December 24, 1981, p. 1, A14.

32. *Washington Post*, January 26, 1982, p. A6; *New York Times*, January 26, 1982, p. B13.

33. *Washington Post*: February 2, 1982, p. B1; February 3, 1982, p. A2; February 4, 1982, p. B1; February 17, 1982, p. B13.

34. *Wall Street Journal*, May 28, 1982. p, 7; *New York Times*: May 28, 1982, p. D15; May 29, 1982, p. 28; June 4, 1982, p. A14; June 16, 1982, p. A26; June 17, 1982, p. A24; *Washington Post*, June 5, 1982, p. A1; June 6, 1982, p. A14; June 7, 1982, p. A4. Berenice Carroll, a historian and participant in some of the grassroots group activities details their activities as well as other uses of direct action in the ERA struggle in "Direct Action and Constitutional Rights: The Case of ERA," *OAH Newsletter*, vol. 11, no. 2 (May 1983): 18–20.

35. *New York Times*, June 8, 1982, p. A25; June 20, 1982, p, 18; *Washington Post*, June 10, 1982, p. A13; June 24, 1982, p. A14, 18.

36. *Washington Post*, June 23, 1982, p. A12; *New York Times*, June 25, 1982, p. 1.

37. *Wall Street Journal*, June 25, 1982, p. 1; Vermont Royster, "The Personhood of Women," *Wall Street Journal*, March 24, 1982, p. 26; Michael Barone, "And a Lot Has Been Won," *Washington Post*, June 28, 1982, p. A12; *Washington Post*, June 25, 1982, p. A2; Pat Schroeder, "ERA: The Fight Isn't Over," *Washington Post*, June 26, 1982, p. A13,

38. *New York Times,* July 1, 1982, p. A12.
39. *Washington Post,* July 15, 1982, p. A5; *New York Times,* July 15, 1982, p. 13.
40. Jane DeHart-Mathews and Donald G. Mathews analyze some of these cultural conflicts in *The Equal Rights Amendment and the Politics of Cultural Conflict: North Carolina, A Case Study* (New York: Oxford University Press, forthcoming); see, also, Edith May and Jerry Frye, "ERA: Postmortem of a Failure in Political Communication," *OAH Newsletter,* vol. 11, no. 3 (August 1983): 21–24; also, see, Jane DeHart Mathews, "The ERA and the Myth of Female Solidarity," (American Historical Association, paper, December 1982).
41. Carol Felsenthal, *The Biography of Phyllis Schlafly, The Sweetheart of the Silent Majority* (Chicago: Regnery Gateway, 1982; originally published by Doubleday, 1981), p. 239.

8. Legal Developments in the Courts and in the States

1. Barbara A. Brown et al., "The Equal Rights Amendment: A Constitutional Basis for Equal Rights," 80 *Yale Law Journal* (1971): 871.
2. *Reed* v. *Reed,* 404 U.S. 71 (1971).
3. *Frontiero* v. *Richardson,* 411 U.S. 677 (1973).
4. *Stanton* v. *Stanton,* 421 U.S. 7 (1975).
5. *Craig* v. *Boren,* 429 U.S. 190, 197 (1976).
6. *Taylor* v. *Louisiana,* 419 U.S. 522 (1975).
7. *Phillips* v. *Martin-Marietta Co.,* 400 U.S. 542 (1971).
8. *Corning Glass Works* v. *Brennan,* 417 U.S. 188 (1974).
9. *Dothard* v. *Rawlinson,* 433 U.S. 321 (1977).
10. *Cleveland Board of Education* v. *LeFleur,* 414 U.S. 632 (1974).
11. *Geduldig* v. *Aiello,* 417 U.S. 484 (1974).
12. *Weinberger* v. *Wiesenfeld,* 420 U.S. 636 (1975); *Califano* v. *Goldfarb,* 430 U.S. 199 (1977).
13. *Los Angeles Dept. of Water & Power* v. *Manhart,* 435 U.S. 702 (1978).
14. *Craig* v. *Boren,* 429 U.S. 190, 197 (1976); *Califano* v. *Webster,* 430 U.S. 313, 316–317 (1977).
15. *Kahn* v. *Shevin,* 416 U.S. 351 (1974); *Schlesinger* v. *Ballard,* 419 U.S. 498 (1980).
16. *Rostker* v. *Goldberg,* 453 U.S. 498 (1975).
17. *Personnel Administrator* v. *Feeney,* 442 U.S, 256 (1979).
18. *Frontiero* v. *Richardson,* 411 U.S. 677 (1973).
19. Janet K. Boles, *The Politics of the Equal Rights Amendment: Conflict and the Decision Process* (New York: Longman, 1979), pp. 107–108.
20. *Roe* v. *Wade,* 410 U.S. 113 (1973); *Doe* v. *Bolton,* 410 U.S. 179 (1973).
21. *Maher* v. *Roe,* 432 U.S. 464 (1977); *Roe* v. *Wade,* 410 U.S. 113 (1973); *Harris* v. *McRae,* 448 U.S. 297 (1980). Schlafly insists that ERA proponents must ensure the impossibility of a reversal of *Harris* v. *McRae* if they ever want an equal rights amendment. The only way they could do that would be to add specific language to the text of ERA to prohibit absolutely any reversal. "Why Congress Must Amend the ERA," *The Phyllis Schlafly Report,* November 1983.
22. *Baker* v. *Nelson,* 191 N.W. 2d 185 (1971). Again Schlafly put the "burden of proof" on opponents to prohibit absolutely any legislation of sexual preference by putting explicit language in ERA. "Why Congress Must Amend the ERA," *The Phyllis Schlafly Report,* November 1983.

23. *Rostker* v. *Goldberg*, 453 U.S. 57 (1980). Citing legal analyses written before *Rostker* was decided, Schlafly asserts that ERA would "make unconstitutional the male-only draft registration law plus the laws exempting women from military combat" without explaining that under *Rostker* the Congress can include women now if it should decide to do so without ERA. "Why Congress Must Amend the ERA," *The Phyllis Schlafly Report*, November 1983.

24. *People* v. *Ellis*, 57 Ill. 2d 127; 311 N.E. 2d 98 (1974). On state ERAs, see generally, ERA Impact Project, a joint project of the NOW Legal Defense and Education Fund and the Women's Law Project (1982) and Dawn Marie Driscoll and Barbara J. Rouse, "Through a Glass Darkly: A Look at State Equal Rights Amendments," 12 *Suffolk Law Review* (Fall 1978): 1282, 1300. Carol Felsenthal, *The Biography of Phyllis Schlafly, The Sweetheart of the Silent Majority* (Chicago: Regnery Gateway, 1982; originally published by Doubleday, 1981), p. 305.

25. *Marcus* v. *Marcus*, 24 Ill. App. 3d 401, 407 (1975); 320 N.E. 2d 581.

26. *Randolph* v. *Dean*, 27 Ill. App. 3d 913; 327 N.E. 2d 473.

27. *Atkinson* v. *Atkinson*, 402 N.E. 2d 831; 82 Ill. App. 3d 617.

28. *Phelps* v. *Bing*, 316 N.E. 775 (1974); 58 Ill. 2d 32.

29. *Steffo* v. *Stanley* 39 Ill. App. 3d 915, 350 N.E. 2d 886 (1976); *Tyrken* v. *Tyrken*, 63 Ill. App. 3d 199; 379 N.E. 2d 804 (1978).

30. *Petrie* v. *Illinois High School Association*, 75 Ill. App. 3d 980, 394 N.E. 2d 855 (1979).

31. *O'Connor* v. *Board of Education*, 645 F.2d 578; 454 U.S. 1085 (1981), *cert. denied*.

32. *People* v. *Ellis*, 57 Ill. 2d 127; 311 N.E. 2d 98 (1974); Illinois Attorney General Opinion in No. S-979 (October 23, 1975) at 9–10.

33. *People* v. *Boyer*, 63 Ill. 2d 433; 349 N.E. 2d 50 (1976); *People* v. *Yocum*, 66 Ill. 2d 211; 361 N.E. 2d 1369 (1977); 431 U.S. 941, *cert. denied*.

34. *People* v. *Medrano*, 24 Ill. App. 3d 429; 321 N.E. 2d 97 (1974).

35. *People* v. *Sherrod*, 50 Ill. App. 3d 552; 365 N.E. 2d 993 (1979).

36. *Wheeler* v. *City of Rockford*, 69 Ill. App. 3d 220; 387 N.E. 2d 358 (1979).

37. Smith-Hurd Illinois Annotated Statutes, Ch. 121–1/2, Sec. 385.1; Ch. 95, Sec. 301, *et seq.*; Ch. 122, Sec. 27–1; 34–18 (Supp. 1980); Ch. 68, Sec. 1–101, *et seq.* (Supp. 1980).

38. Utah Constitution, Art. 4, Sec. 1 (1896).

39. Utah Constitution, Art. 16, Sec. 8 (1933).

40. Utah Constitution, Art. 16, Sec. 3 (1980).

41. *Cox* v. *Cox*, 532 P.2d 994 (1975),

42. *Stanton* v. *Stanton*, 517 P.2d 1010 (1974). But see *Stanton* v. *Stanton*, 421 U.S. 7 (1975), also 522 P.2d 112 (1976), and 429 U.S. 59 (1977), "per curiam".

43. *In re Estate of Armstrong*, 440 P.2d 881 (1968).

44. *Kopp* v. *Salt Lake City*, 506 P.2d 809 (1973).

45. *Turner* v. *Department of Employment Security*, 531 P.2d 870 (1975); 423 U.S. 44 (1975), "per curiam".

46. Virginia Constitution, Art. 1, Sec. 11 (1971).

47. Driscoll and Rouse, "Through a Glass Darkly," pp. 1282, 1300.

48. *Craig* v. *Boren*, 429 U.S. 190 (1976).

49. *Archer and Johnson* v. *Mayes*, 213 Va. 633; 194 S.E.2d 707 (1973) at 708.

50. Virginia Code, Sec. 20–61 (Replacement Vol. 1977); Virginia Code, Sec. 20–91 (Replacement Vol. 1975); Virginia Code, Sec. 59.1–21.19 (Cumulative Supplement, 1980), Sec. 36–90 (Replacement Vol. 1976), Virginia Code, Sec. 38.1–381.5 (Cumulative Supplement, 1980); Virginia Code,

Sec.55–47.1 (Replacement Vol. 1980), Sec. 18.2–61 (Replacement Vol. 1976), Sec. 64.1–5.1–5.2 (Replacement Vol. 1980).

51. *Plas* v. *State*, 598 P.2d 966 (1979); Alaska Constitution, Art. 1, Sec. 3 (1972); Alaska Statutes of 1962, Sec. 23.10.155 (Michie 1972 Pamphlet), Sec. 1.5511e 205 (Michie 1980 Cumulative Supplement), Sec. 18.80.210, 230; Alaska Statutes 18.80.220, 240, 250 (Michie 1974 Pamphlet).

52. Colorado Constitution, Art. II, Sec. 29 (1972); Colorado Revised Statutes 1973, 86–110, *et seq.*, 31–30.601 *et seq.* (1978 Cumulative Supplement); Colorado Revised Statutes 24–34–402, 24–34–502, 24–34–602, 5–1–109, 24–50–141 (1983 Replacement Volume); *People* v. *Salinas*, 551 P.2d 703 (1976); *People* v. *Green*, 514 P.2d 769 (1973).

53. *Holdman* v. *Olim*, 581 P.2d 1164 (1978); Sherry Broder and Beverly Wee, "Hawaii's Equal Rights Amendment: Its Impact on Athletic Opportunities and Competition for Women," 2 *Hawaii Law Review* 97, 111 (Winter 1979).

54. Connecticut Constitution, Art. I, Sec. 20 (1974); Connecticut General Statutes, 4–61. t-w; 31–12–19; 53–35; Connecticut General Statutes, 36–436 *et seq.* (1979 Rev.), 46b–40 *et seq.* (1979 Rev.), 53a–65; *Page* v. *Welfare Commissioner*, 365 A.2d 1118 (1976).

55. Maryland Constitution, Art. 46 (1972); *Kline* v. *Ansell*, 414 A.2d 929 (1980); *Rand* v. *Rand*, 280 Md. 508, 374 A.2d 900 (1977); Maryland Code, Art. 72A, Sec. 1 (Cumulative Supplement, 1977); Maryland Code, Art. 49B, Sec. 16(a) (1979 Replacement Volume), Art. 100, Sec. 55A, 55B. Maryland Code, (Replacement Volume 1979), Art. 493, 19a; Art. 100, 82e, 11(b)(9), (c)(1) and (2); Art. 100, 21(b); Art. 48A, 354F, 477J.

56. Massachusetts Constitution, Part I, Art. I (1976); *Commonwealth* v. *King*, 372 N.E.2d 196 (Mass. Sup. Jud. 1977). Massachusetts General Legislative Acts, Ch. 208, Sec. 34; Ch. 273, Sec. 3c 208, Sec. 12, 13, 20, 20A; Ch. 188, Sec. 1, 3, 4, 6, 7, 8; Ch. 30, Sec. 2628; Ch. 121 B, Sec. 1, 3, 4; Ch. 117, Sec. 3; Ch. 118, Sec. 3; Ch. 208, Sec. 1; Ch. 273, Sec. 1, 15; Ch. 272, Sec. 7; Ch. 15, Sec. 1A, 1E, 20A; Ch. 17, Sec. 14; Ch. 19, Sec. 15; Ch. 23A, Sec. 4; Ch. 122, Sec. 2; Ch. 272, Sec. 1, *et seq.*; Ch. 209, Sec. 1.

57. Montana Constitution, Art. II, Sec. 4 (1973); *State* v. *Craig*, 545 P.2d 649 (1976). Revised Code of Montana, 10–301–10–310 (1947), 23–3027; 75–8704; 83–3–3 (1947) and repealing 36–102 (1947); Montana Code Annotated, 40–2–102; 40–4–203; 40–4–204; 40–4–212; 45–5–503; 49–2–306, 49–3; 39–7–203 (1979).

58. New Hampshire Constitution, Part I, Art. II (1974); *Buckner* v. *Buckner*, 415 A.2d 871 (1980). New Hampshire Revised Statutes Annotated, Sec. 275.15, 275.17; 457.4; 460:1; 460.3; 458.7 (VIII); 458.7(XI); (Replacement Vol. 1977) 458.7 (XIII); 458.7 (XII); 164–A:1(II).

59. *Schaab* v. *Schaab*, 531 P.2d 954 (1974) and *Futrell* v. *Ahrens*, 540 P.2d 214 (1975); New Mexico Constitution, Art. II, Sec. 18 (1973); Attorney General Opinion No. 75–75 at 196 (12/24/75), No. 95–16 at 59 (2/21/75); New Mexico Statutes Annotated, Sec. 40–1–5, 4–1, 4–7, 3–7, 3–13, 3–8, 3–9, 3–12 (1978); New Mexico Statutes Annotated, 40–A–9–21, Sec. 30–2–7 (1978).

The Code review was published in seven law review articles: Leo Kanowitz, "The New Mexico Equal Rights Amendment: Introduction and Overview," 3 *New Mexico Law Review* 1 (January 1973); Anne K. Bingaman, "The Effects of an Equal Rights Amendment on the New Mexico System of Community Property: Problems of Characterization, Management, and Control", 3 *New Mexico Law Review* 11 (January 1973); Willis H. Ellis, "Equal Rights and the Debt Provisions of New Mexico Community Property Law", 3 *New Mexico Law*

Review 57 (January 1973); Kendall O. Schlenker, "Tax Implications of the Equal Rights Amendment," 3 *New Mexico Law Review* 69 (January 1973); Joseph Goldberg and Mariclaire Hale, "The Equal Rights Amendment and the Administration of Income Assistance Programs in New Mexico," 3 *New Mexico Law Review* 84 (January 1973); Charles Daniels, "The Impact of the Equal Rights Amendment on the New Mexico Criminal Code," 3 *New Mexico Law Review* 106 (January 1973); Jennie D. Behles and Daniel J. Behles, "Equal Rights in Divorce and Separation," 3 *New Mexico Law Review* 118 (January 1973).

60. Pennsylvania Constitution, Art. I, Sec. 28 (1971); see, for example, *Commonwealth* v. *Butler*, 328 A.2d 851, 458 Pa. 289, and Margaret K. Krasik, "Comment: A Review of the Implementation of the Pennsylvania Equal Rights Amendment," 14 *Duquesne Law Rev.* 683 (1976); *Henderson* v. *Henderson*, 458 Pa. 97, 101; 327 A.2d 60, 62 (1974) "per curiam."

61. Texas Constitution, Art. 1, Sec. 3a (1972); *Mercer* v. *Board of Trustees*, 538 S.W.2d 201 (Texas Cir. App. 1976); Texas Family Code Annotated, Sec. 4.02 and 12.011 (Vernon, 1975), Sections 4.02, 3.59 (Vernon Supplement 1980); Texas Penal Code Annotated, Sec. 25.05 (Vernon, 1974); Texas Probate Code Annotated, Sec. 109(a), 271 (Vernon, 1980).

62. Washington Constitution, Art. 31, Sec. 1 (1972); *Darrin* v. *Gould*, 540 P.2d 885 (1975), 85 Wash. 2d 859, at 889; *Marchioro* v. *Chaney*, 582 P.2d 487, 491 (1978).

63. Wyoming Constitution, Art. 1, Sec. 2, 3, Art. VI, Sec. 1 (1890); Wyoming Statutes, Title 276–101(b), 102 (1977), Title 27–6–106 (1977).

9. Losing Consensus in the Congress

1. H.J. Res. 1, 98th Cong., 1st sess., January 3, 1983, 236 cosponsors; S.J. Res. 10, 98th Cong., 1st sess., January 25, 1983, 55 cosponsors; *New York Times*, January 28, 1983; Author's conversations with NOW and NWPC officials, including Kathy Wilson and Judy Goldsmith during 1983; Judy Mann, "ERA Again," *Washington Post*, January 6, 1983, B1; James J. Kilpatrick, "ERA is Back, Warts and All," *Washington Post*, January 26, 1983; Pamela Johnston Conover and Virginia Gray, *Feminism and the New Right* (New York: Praeger Publishers, 1983), pp. 200–202.

2. House Judiciary Subcommittee on Civil and Constitutional Rights Hearings June 15, 1983 and July 13, 1983; Senate Judiciary Subcommittee on the Constitution, Hearings May 26, 1983; *Washington Post*, May 27, 1983, p. A17; *New York Times*, May 27, 1983, p. A11; Phyllis Schlafly, "ERA is Redundant, Will Create Problems," *USA Today*, May 23, 1983; "Why Congress Must Amend the ERA," *The Phyllis Schlafly Report*, November 1983.

3. *Washington Post*, November 16, 1983, p. 1; Patricia Schroeder, "Parliamentary Push for ERA Was Not So Shocking," *Wall Street Journal*, December 13, 1983, p. 30.

4. Conversations with national officials of NOW and NWPC,including Judy Goldsmith and Kathy Wilson, November 1983.

5. 129 *Congressional Record*, H9849–50 (daily edition, November 15, 1983).

6. 129 *Congressional Record*, H9835, H9836, H9841, H9857, H9861 (daily edition, November 15, 1983).

7. 129 *Congressional Record*, H9836–7 (daily edition, November 15, 1983).

8. 129 *Congressional Record*, H9836–7 (daily edition, November 15, 1983).

9. 129 *Congressional Record*, H9862–3 (daily edition, November 15, 1983).

10. 129 *Congressional Record*, H9846, H9852 (daily edition, November 15, 1983).

11. 129 *Congressional Record*, H9854 (daily edition, November 15, 1983).

12. 129 *Congressional Record*, H9840, H9856. H9841–3 (daily edition, Nov. 15, 1983); *Washington Post*, November 15, 1983.

13. 129 *Congressional Record*, H9851, H9852, H9853, (daily edition, Nov. 15, 1983).

14. 129 *Congressional Record*, H9865, (daily edition, Nov. 15, 1983); *New York Times*, November 15, 1983, p. 1; *Washington Post*, November 16, 1983, p. 1.

15. 129 *Congressional Record*, H9857 (daily edition, November 15, 1983).

16. 129 *Congressional Record*, H9865 (daily edition, Nov. 15, 1983).

17. Boles, *The Politics of the Equal Rights Amendment: Conflict and the Decision Process* (New York: Longman, 1979), pp. 2–3.

18. *Wall Street Journal*, November 16, 1983, p. 2; interviews with NOW and NWPC leaders, including Judy Goldsmith and Kathy Wilson.

19. 129 *Congressional Record*, H9835–41, H9857, H9861, H9836–7, H9862–3 (daily edition, November 15, 1983).

20. Hearing before the House Subcommittee on Commerce, Transportation, and Tourism on the Non-Discrimination in Insurance Act of 1983, 98th Cong., 1st sess., February 22 and 24, 1983, No. 98–35.

21. 129 *Congressional Record*, E4389 (daily edition, Sept. 20, 1983); 129 *Congressional Record*, H9354 (daily edition, Nov. 8, 1983); 129 *Congressional Record*, H9704 (daily edition, Nov. 10, 1984); Hearings Before the Senate Committee on Finance, 98th Cong., 2d sess., January 24 and 26, 1984, Senate Doc. 98–673.

22. 129 *Congressional Record*, H9088 (daily edition, Nov. 2, 1983); Hearing Before the Senate Committee on Finance, 98th Cong., 2d sess., on the Retirement Equity Act of 1984, August 6, 1984, Senate Report 98–575.

23. 129 *Congressional Record*, H45 (daily edition, January 23, 1984).

24. *Spaulding* v. *University of Washington*, 740 F.2d 686 (9th Circuit 1984) *cert. denied* 105 S.Ct. 511 (1984); *Griggs* v. *Duke Power*, 401 U.S. 424 (1971). See also, *County of Washington* v. *Gunther*, 452 U.S. 161 (1981); *American Federation of State, County, and Municipal Employees* v. *State of Washington*, 578 F.Supp. 846 (W.D. Washington, 1983).

25. Statement of Clarence Pendleton, *Employment and Training Reporter*, No. 12 (Manpower Information, Inc.), Nov. 28, 1984, p. 306–9; *New York Times*, December 14, 1984, p. A2O; Associated Press wire story, November 17, 1984; June O'Neill, "An Argument Against Comparable Worth," in U.S. Commission on Civil Rights: *Comparable Worth: Issue for the '80's, A Consultation of the U.S. Commission on Civil Rights, June 6–7, 1984*, vol. 1, p. 177.

26. *New York Times*, November 25, 1984, p. 1; letter to the editor from Congresswoman Mary Rose Oakar, *Washington Post*, December 15, 1984, p. A27.

27. *Hishon* v. *King and Spaulding*, 81 L.Ed 2d 59 (1984); *Grove City College* v. *Bell*, 79 L. Ed. 2d 516 (1984).

28. *Arizona Governing Committee for Tax Deferred Corporations*, v. *Norris*, 103 S.Ct. 3492 (1983); *Spirt* v. *Teachers Insurance and Annuity Association*, 691 F.2d 1054 (1984); TIAA/CREF, Associated Press wire story, October 9, 1984.

29. *Roberts, et al.* v. *United States Jaycees*, 82 L.Ed. 2d 462 (1984).

30. *Firefighters Local Union No. 1784* v. *Stotts*, 104 S.Ct. 2576 (1984).

31. *Fischer* v. *Dept. of Public Welfare*, 482 A.2d 1137; 482 A.2d 1148 (1984);

Hartford Accident & Indemnity Co. v. *Insurance Commissioner*, 482 A.2d 542 (1984).

32. *Grove City College* v. *Bell*, 79 L.Ed. 2d 516 (1984).

33. *Women's Political Times*, IX, no. 5 (August/Sept. 1984): 11; Conversations with Jesse Jackson, Judy Goldsmith, and Kathy Wilson, Spring and Summer 1984; *New York Times*, July 19, 1984, p. A21.

34. *National NOW Times*, vol.XVII, no. 4 (July/August 1984): 1; *Women's Political Times* (August/Sept. 1984): 1; also, conversations with Kathy Wilson, Blandina Cardenas Ramirez, as well as personal observations at the NOW 1984 convention and the Democratic National Convention in San Francisco, 1984.

35. *National NOW Times*, vol. XVII, no. 4 (July/August 1984): 5–6; conversations with Alice Travis, Kathy Wilson, Judy Goldsmith, Jesse Jackson, Shirley Chisholm, C. Delores Tucker, and Doris Crenshaw at the Democratic National Convention, 1984.

36. *Washington Post*, August 22, 1984, p. B2; August 14, 1984, p. A6; *Women's Political Times* (August/Sept. 1984): 1.

37. *Washington Post*, February 21, 1985, p. C3.

38. *New York Times*, November 14, 1984, p. A22.

39. Data collected by the Women's Campaign Fund and National Women's Political Caucus, Susan Hildebrandt; *National NOW Times* (Nov/Dec. 1984): 1-2; *Wall Street Journal*, December 31, 1984, p. 34.

40. *Washington Post*, March 3, 1985, p. 5; *New York Times*, February 17, 1985, p. A6.

41. Andrew Hacker, "Women v. Men in the Work Force," *New York Times Magazine*, December 9, 1984, p. 124–129; *New York Times*, December 9, 1984, p. 2E.

42. *National NOW Times* (January/February 1985): 3; *New York Times*, January 18, 1985, p. A14; *Congressional Quarterly*, January 26, 1985, p. 8.

43. *Congressional Quarterly*, January 26, 1985, p. 43.

44. *Congressional Quarterly*, January 26, 1985, pp. 8–10.

45. *New York Times*, July 6, 1985, p. 44; author's observations at NWPC Convention, June 30, 1985, in Atlanta.

46. *Washington Post*, July 22, 1985, p. A10, A8; July 23, 1985, p. A5; *New York Times*, July 27, 1985, p. 48.

Index

MARY FRANCES BERRY, Professor of History and Law at Howard University and a member of the U. S. Commission on Civil Rights, is author of *Black Resistance/White Law: A History of Constitutional Racism in America*; *Military Necessity and Civil Rights Policy: Black Citizenship and the Constitution, 1861–1868*; and coauthor of *Long Memory: The Black Experience in America*.